TASTE

Why You Like What You Like

A Cultural Studies Analysis

by

Arthur Asa Berger
San Francisco State University

Illustrated by the Author

Series in Sociology
VERNON PRESS

In the Americas:
Vernon Press
1000 N West Street, Suite 1200,
Wilmington, Delaware 19801
United States

In the rest of the world:
Vernon Press
C/Sancti Espiritu 17,
Malaga, 29006
Spain

Series in Sociology

Library of Congress Control Number: 2022950350

ISBN: 978-1-64889-713-9

Also available: 978-1-64889-588-3 [Hardback]; 978-1-64889-644-6 [PDF, E-Book]

Illustrated with drawings and photographs by the author.

Cover design by Vernon Press.

Table of Contents

Dirk von Lehn
King's College London

Sociology reveals that the idea of personal opinion (like the idea of personal taste) is an illusion. From this, it is concluded that sociology is reductive, that it disenchants, that it demobilizes people by taking away all their illusions....If it is true that the idea of personal opinion itself is socially determined, that it is a product of history reproduced by education, that our opinions are determined, then it is better to know this; and if we have some chance of having personal opinions, it is perhaps on condition that we know our opinions are not spontaneously so.

Pierre Bourdieu. *Sociology in Question.* (1993).

Whereas the ideology of charisma regards taste in legitimate culture as a gift of nature, scientific observation shows that cultural needs are the product of upbringing and education: surveys establish that all cultural practices (museum visits, concert going, reading, etc.), and preferences in literature, painting or music, are closely linked to educational level (measured by qualifications or length of schooling) and secondarily to social origin.

Pierre Bourdieu. *Distinction: A Social Critique of the Judgement of Taste.*

Acknowledgments

I owe a debt of gratitude to all the semioticians, psychoanalysts, sociologists, Marxists, journalists, and others whose writings I have used and discussed in this book. I also appreciate the support and help of my editor, Blanca Caro Duran, and the production staff at Vernon Press for their work on this book. Finally, I want to thank Greg Rowland, an Oxford-trained semiotician, for contributing his analysis of the semiotics of taste to this book. Note: A relatively small amount of material is based on my previous writings.

Dedication

In memory of my two uncles, Philip Fishman and Jacob Savel, who spent endless hours debating whether Brooks Brothers or J. Press was the better brand of clothing for men of good taste.

List of Figures and Tables

Figures

Tables

Takeaways

This book discusses the ideas of (and offers brief quotations from) key texts written by some of the most important thinkers who have concerned themselves with taste, in the broadest sense of the term. Readers of this book will not only have learned about their ideas but also been able to see how they expressed themselves. Here are some of the most important takeaways; many are also briefly discussed in the glossary:

Pierre Bourdieu was a French sociologist whose 1997 book, *Distinction: A Social Critique of the Judgement of Taste,* is considered one of the most important sociology books published in the twentieth century. It deals with the relationship between socio-economic class and cultural consumption and taste. Bourdieu argues, in essence, that taste is socially constructed and shaped by many factors, such as the family in which a person is raised, the family's social status, and related concerns.

Ferdinand de Saussure is one of the founding fathers of semiotics, the science of signs. He defined a sign as a combination of a signifier (a sound or object) and a signified (the meaning of the sign), adding that the relationship that existed between signifiers and signified is conventional and can change over time. His book, *Course in General Linguistics*, is one of the foundational texts in semiotics.

The theories of the French philosopher **Michel Foucault**, about the codes that shape culture and about his ideas about power being ubiquitous and part of all human interactions. Foucault is one of the most important and influential thinkers of recent years and the author of many books, such as *The Order of Things: An Archaeology of the Human Sciences.*

A study by an important psychoanalyst, **Erik Erikson,** which considers the difficulties adolescents face as they grow up. He discusses this topic in his book, *Childhood and Society.* Erikson argues that people all have to confront eight developmental crises, such as initiative and guilt in childhood, and positively resolve them all if they are to avoid psychological problems.

The work of an important psychoanalytic theorist, **Joan Riviere,** who has interesting things to say about the trauma babies have when breastfeeding and about greed and our desire for things as proof that we are worthy of love. Her essay is part of a book, *Love, Hate and Reparation* that has a second essay by Melanie Klein.

Milton Sapirstein, an American psychiatrist, wrote a book, *Paradoxes of Everyday Life,* that dealt with the paradoxical aspects of everyday life from a psychoanalytic perspective. The book has chapters on topics such as screaming mothers, neurotic children from happy families, and male infidelity.

Melanie Klein, a controversial psychoanalytic theorist, discusses the experiences babies have when breastfeeding and other topics and argues that people often continually go through the cycle of loving, hating, and making reparations.

In his 1971 book, *Beyond Laughter,* **Martin Grotjahn** offers a psychoanalytic perspective on detective stories, horror stories, humor, and many other aspects of popular culture and everyday life.

The British-American poet, **W. H. Auden**, is considered to be one of the greatest poets of the twentieth century. His poems often dealt with ethics and political concerns.

An English anthropologist, **Geoffrey Gorer**, wrote from a psychoanalytic perspective and analyzed the way Great Russians raised their babies in his book *The People of Great Russia: A Psychological Study.* Gorer argued that the use of swaddling for babies by the Great Russians led to them being extreme in terms of their attitudes towards gratifications when adults.

The theories of another psychoanalyst, and marketing consultant, **Clotaire Rapaille,** on what he calls *The Culture Code,* which explains how children from the age of one to seven become "imprinted" by the codes of their culture and this imprinting stays with them throughout their lives. Rapaille shows how people from various countries differ from one another in terms of the codes that shape their cultures and taste preferences.

A study by an important psychoanalyst, **Erik Erikson,** which considers the difficulties adolescents face as they grow up. He discusses this topic in his book, *Childhood and Society.* Erikson argues that all people have to confront eight developmental crises, such as initiative and guilt in childhood, and positively resolve them all if they are to avoid psychological problems.

Gerald Zaltman, a professor of marketing at Harvard University Business School, is the author of *How Consumers Think: Essential Insights into the Mind of the Market* (2003), which asserts that ninety percent of our thinking takes place in our unconscious. He also discusses the role that metaphors play in marketing.

The theories of **Sigmund Freud** and his hypothesis about the three levels of the psyche: consciousness, the subconscious, and the unconscious. Freud believed we cannot know the contents of the unconscious, but must recognize that it affects much of our thinking and behavior. Freud was one of the most important psychologists and influenced many generations of psychologists and psychoanalysts.

There are many kinds of Marxists who interpret his writings in a variety of ways, but all agree that **Karl Marx** was one of the most important thinkers, whose ideas have played an enormous role in recent historical experience and in social and political thought. Many of the thinkers discussed in this book were influenced by Marxist thought.

Erich Fromm writes about narcissism in his book, *The Greatness and Limitations of Freud's Thought,* and suggests that narcissism, if not excessive, has a survival value. Fromm has a theory about what he calls "social character" which is found in groups and different nations. This social character shapes much of our behavior and makes people "act as they have to act." This suggests that social character is, in subtle ways, coercive.

In his book, *The Alienation of Modern Man,* published in 1959, the German Marxist, **Fritz Pappenheim,** deals with alienation in the novels of Franz Kafka, Thomas Wolfe, and Arthur Miller and with the impact of alienation on American culture and society.

Wolfgang Haug, a German Marxist, is the author of *Critique of Commodity Aesthetics: Appearance, Sexuality and Advertising in Capitalist Society* (1986), which argues that the advertising industry, a servant of capitalism, has learned how to mold and exploit human sexuality and alter human need and instinct structures. Aesthetics, then, have social and political significance.

Georg Simmel, a German sociologist, wrote about many aspects of everyday life such as fashion, people's attitudes toward money, and travel. His writings on aesthetics, methodology, and other sociological concerns have been influential.

Collective Search for Identity (1969) is the title of a book by sociologist **Orrin Klapp,** that deals with identity-seeking movements in American society. The book investigates fads, fashions, cultic movements, heroes, and celebrities in terms of what they reveal about people's search for an identity in a mass society, such as the United States.

Aaron Wildavsky was a professor of political science at the University of California, Berkeley, and the author of numerous books and articles about politics. His fields of expertise involved budgeting and political culture. He worked, at the end of his career, with the English social-anthropologist Mary Douglas on grid-group theory.

Judith Butler, the author of a celebrated work, *Gender Trouble: Feminism and the Subversion of Identity,* argues that gender is best understood to be a performance, and the binary distinction, male or female, is too limited. Gender, she argues, is not biologically "fixed" but is socially constructed. This idea is now widely accepted by gender scholars.

Herbert Gans, a sociologist, wrote what we might describe as a defense of popular culture in his book, *Popular Culture and High Culture: An Evaluation of Taste* (1974). He suggested that America has five different "taste cultures" with different aesthetic standards but all of equal worth. These "taste cultures" are connected to socio-economic status and different levels of aesthetic sophistication.

Claritas is a marketing company that argues that there are more than sixty categories or clusters of consumers, all quite different, who can be targeted by advertising agencies and marketing departments. Claritas gives each cluster jazzy names such as "upper crust," "young digerati," "Urban Elders," and "Bedrock America." These clusters tend to live in the same zip codes because, as Claritas puts it, "birds of a feather tend to flock together."

In his role as a public intellectual, sociologist **Todd Gitlin** wrote about various topics related to contemporary American culture and society, with a focus on politics and the media. He was a professor at Columbia University in New York.

W. Lloyd Warner was a sociologist, who explained that there were six social classes in America: the upper-upper, lower-upper, upper-middle, lower-middle, upper-lower, and lower-lower. His breakdown still is fairly accurate. The "common" person in America, he suggested, comes from the upper-lower and lower-middle classes. His work calls attention to one of the most important problems American society faces, which involves the different social classes and the gross distortion of wealth in America, and the problems that inequality brings.

Myth, it is suggested, plays an important role in shaping much of our behavior, even though we are not aware that this is the case. This book offers a "myth model," which shows how given myths can be found in historical experience, psychoanalytic theory, elite culture, popular culture, and everyday life. In the Western world, one of our most important myths is the story (myth) of Adam and Eve in the Garden of Eden.

Jean-Francois Lyotard is the author of *The Postmodern Condition* (1984) which argues that postmodernism has led to the rejection of the grand philosophical systems that people once used to make sense of life (such as belief in progress) and now have to deal with many competing narratives leading to a crisis in legitimation.

A British Marxist communications scholar, **Raymond Williams**, discussed the role of ideology in the media and also popularized and explained Antonio

Gramsci's theories about hegemony and domination. Because hegemony is all-pervasive, Williams argued, people do not realize they have been indoctrinated with belief systems advantageous to the ruling classes in capitalist societies.

The discussion of **socio-economic classes in Britain**, based on a survey by the British Broadcasting System, reveals not six classes, as found in W. Lloyd Warner's typology for American society, but seven, described as Elites (6%), Established Middle Class (25%), Technical Middle Class (6%), New Affluent Workers (15%), Emergent Service Workers (19%), Traditional Working Class (14%), and the Precariat or most deprived (15%).

Postmodernism is the subject of considerable debate among culture theorists: how do we define it, what impact has it had on America and other countries, and does it still exist, or have we moved beyond it to post-postmodernism? Jean-François Lyotard's book, *The Postmodern Condition*, defines postmodernism as "incredulity towards meta-narratives." What this means and how postmodernism has affected society and social relations continues to be an enigmatic matter.

One of the more important theorists of postmodernism, **Jean Baudrillard,** has argued that "reality itself is hyperrealist" or that reality has been replaced by hyperreality. Thus, for example, Disneyland is real and America, Baudrillard argues, is hyperreal. As he explained, "America is neither dream nor reality. It is hyperreality."

The British social anthropologist, **Mary Douglas**, developed what she called Grid-Group theory, which focuses on the strength or weakness of boundaries around groups and the number of rules to which they are subjected. She argues that Grid-Group theory led to our recognizing four "lifestyles" that play an enormous role in people's lives—even though members of a lifestyle might not recognize that they belong to one. Her theory suggests that many of our taste preferences are shaped by the lifestyles to which we belong.

Umberto Eco was an Italian semiotician who also wrote some very popular novels, one of which, *The Name of the Rose*, was made into a film. He wrote books on semiotic theory and the application of semiotics to literature and popular culture. His book, *A Theory of Semiotics*, is considered a classic. He explained that signs can be used to lie and explained that if signs cannot be used to lie, they cannot be used at all.

Yuri Lotman, a Russian semiotician, wrote numerous books on the semiotics of culture and on the arts, including one on cinema. He explained that everything in a work of art is important and that works of art are extremely concentrated. They contain an enormous amount of information in a small text, which transmits different information to readers based on their ability to comprehend the text. He founded a school of semiotics that focused on using semiotics to understand culture.

Mikhail Bakhtin was a Russian semiotician who argued that works of art always have connections to previous works of art, what semioticians call intertextuality. Sometimes the connection is overt, as in the "1984" Macintosh commercial and George Orwell's *1984*, and sometimes it is not recognized by the artists who create texts. Bakhtin was also interested in humor and the role of laughter in societies and politics. He saw laughter as a "liberating" force.

Ruth Rubinstein taught sociology at the Fashion Institute of Technology of the State University of New York. Her book, *Dress Codes: Meanings and Messages in American Culture* (1995), is a semiotic study of fashion that shows how clothing and dress play an important role in American culture.

In his book, *The Theming of America: Dreams, Visions, and Commercial Spaces* (1997), sociologist **Mark Gottdiener** offers a semiotically informed study of themed environments, such as malls and Disneyland, that explores their impact on American society and culture.

The French Marxist semiotician, **Roland Barthes**, was interested in ideologies hidden in mass culture and everyday experiences and wrote an influential book, *Mythologies*, about masked ideologies in everyday life in French culture. He wrote many books on different aspects of semiotics, including a semiotic study of Japanese culture titled, *Empire of Signs*. In that book, he wrote about Japanese chopsticks, Japanese food, bowing, and other aspects of Japanese culture and everyday life.

A British semiotician, **Daniel Chandler**, wrote one of the most important explanations of semiotic theory, *Semiotics: the Basics*, which also functions as a leading textbook on the subject. It also has the virtue of being both comprehensive and highly readable. Chandler writes about the importance of codes and explains that we need to know codes in order to make sense of signs and that aesthetic codes play an important role in shaping our preferences.

Preface

Dirk von Lehn

King's College London

Scholars from a wide range of disciplines have written about "taste." In this literature, the opinions about taste, where it origins and is located, and how it is produced, by whom and for what ends, vary a lot. The commonly held view is that taste is subjective. This is most evidently expressed in the saying that "beauty is in the eye of the beholder."

In this delightful introduction to "Taste," Arthur Berger covers discussions about the subjectivity of taste, yet, throughout the book shows that taste is a multidimensional category. He covers taste from the perspectives of "semiotics," "psychology"/"psycho-analysis," "sociology," and "politics"/"Marxist Theory." Thus, Berger gives us a flavor of how the perspective we adopt, determines if we perceive taste as being derived from the interpretation of signs, the subjective dispositions, social influences, or power relationships.

With Berger's book, readers coming afresh to discussions about "taste" from their particular disciplinary point of view have the opportunity to discover alternative perspectives on "taste", and to reflect on their own perspective on "taste" by learning about other points of view. The discovery of other perspectives is facilitated and eased by mangy illustrative examples that bring the theories to life. With that, Berger makes theories of "taste" accessible and the learning about these theories an enjoyable experience.

Part I:
Culture Theory and Taste

No judgment of taste is innocent. In a word, we are all snobs. **Pierre Bourdieu** brilliantly illuminates this situation of the middle class in the modern world. France's leading sociologist focuses here on the French bourgeoisie, its tastes, and preferences. *Distinction* is at once a vast ethnography of contemporary France and a dissection of the bourgeois mind.

In the course of everyday life, people constantly choose between what they find aesthetically pleasing and what they consider tacky, merely trendy, or ugly. Bourdieu bases his study on surveys that took into account the multitude of social factors that play a part in a French person's choice of clothing, furniture, leisure activities, dinner menus for guests, and many other matters of taste. What emerges from his analysis is that social snobbery is everywhere in the bourgeois world. The different aesthetic choices people make are all distinctions—that is, choices made in opposition to those made by other classes. Taste is not pure. Bourdieu finds a world of social meaning in the decision to order bouillabaisse, in our contemporary cult of thinness, in the "California sports" such as jogging and cross-country skiing. The social world, he argues, functions simultaneously as a system of power relations and as a symbolic system in which minute distinctions of taste become the basis for social judgment.

The topic of Bourdieu's book is a fascinating one: the strategies of social pretension are always curiously engaging. But the book is more than fascinating. It is a major contribution to current debates on the theory of culture and a challenge to the major theoretical schools in contemporary sociology.

https://www.hup.harvard.edu/catalog.php?isbn=9780674212770

Introduction:
What is Taste?

Taste is an enigmatic topic. We recognize that taste plays an important role in our life, in that everything we buy and many things we do are governed by our sense of taste, but what exactly is taste?

How do we get our sense of taste and how does it affect our everyday lives? Does it develop as we grow older or is it a constant in our lives?

Is it affected by all the "influencers" to whom we are exposed as we watch TikTok and commercials, or do influencers merely spark some kind of inner sense of taste that was with us all the time? Is our taste based on our social and economic status or something else?

What roles do income and cost have in determining what we choose to buy? What roles do the qualities of what we buy and the choices we make shape our decisions? Is taste based on logical thinking about things we wish to do or buy or on emotions generated in us by things like identification, status, or cultural imperatives? Taste always involves some element of choice, because if there is no choice, taste is irrelevant or moot. But what are the determinants when we compare things to buy or get or do when we have choices to make?

This book takes its point of departure from the work of the French sociologist Pierre Bourdieu, whose book *Distinction* is considered a classic work of sociological analysis. I've read his book and several others he wrote and that led me to decide to write a book on taste.

Figure 0.1: The Mercedes™ Star

Let me begin by posing a problem about choice and taste when it comes to purchasing an automobile.

Taste and Buying a New Car

I will begin with a problem, relating to taste, that many people face: purchasing an automobile. The average cost for a new car in the U.S.A. in 2022 is around $47,000. Suppose you wish to purchase an automobile for around $45,000. For around that amount of money, if you like German cars, you can buy one of the following cars:

Mercedes Benz A-Class
Audi A3
BMW

and many other less expensive cars that can end up costing around $45,000 if you add various refinements to them. What is it, we may ask, that leads someone to purchase a Mercedes Benz instead of an Audi or a BMW if they all cost the same amount of money?

If you needed a new car, operating upon pure logic, you would consult *Consumer Reports* and see what its engineers suggest you purchase, based on the car's reliability, safety features, gas mileage, and various other considerations. You could then decide to buy a Honda Civic or a Toyota Corolla for around $21,000 (or one of their similarly priced competitors) and use the money you save by doing so for other things, such as repairing your house, taking a vacation, or whatever. You could also consult the *Consumer Reports* rating for the three German cars and that might affect your choice of the car.

But our taste and the decisions we make based on our taste (and I believe we all recognize this is the case) are not always based on rational thinking and logic. In fact, much and perhaps most of our decision-making is not primarily based on logic but upon emotion.

Do people buy this or that brand and model of a car because they are getting a great "deal" on the car? Because of its status? Because they like the design of the car? Because they like the color of the car? Because a friend has that car? Because someone they look up to has that car? Because it is all they can afford? Because it got an excellent review in *Consumer Reports*? Or for some combination of these reasons.

Some of the best minds in marketing have devoted an enormous amount of time, money, and energy trying to figure out why Jane Smith or John Doe buys a Mercedes instead of a BMW or a Porsche or buys a Toyota Corolla instead of a Honda Civic, or why anyone buys a Jeep Wrangler or a Fiat.

Human beings are very complicated creatures, and our behavior continues to puzzle scholars, scientists, and marketers interested in finding out why people do what they do.

Figure 0.2: Advertisement for a Porsche™

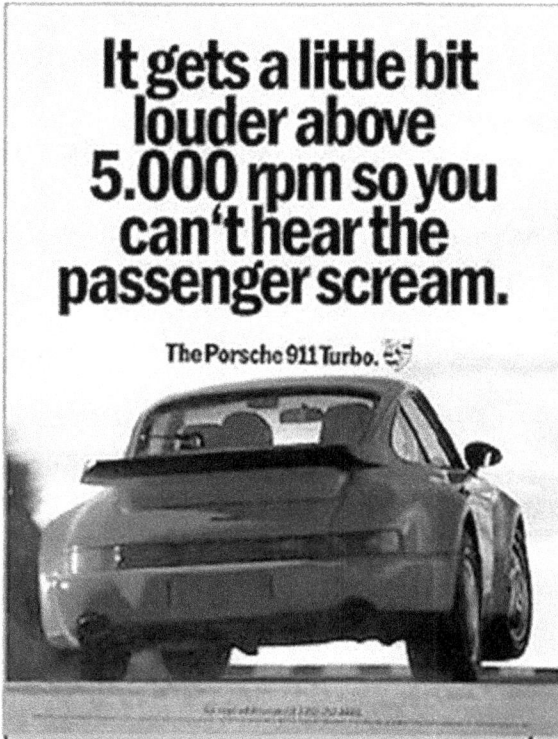

This advertisement appeals to people who love speed and a sense of power, and have around $250,000 to spend on a car.

"De gustibus non est disputandum" means "There is no accounting for taste." I may not be able to account for taste—that is, explain why people have the taste they have for this or that food, object, or anything, but I can offer some insights that tell us something about how people, in general, arrive at their taste preferences.

A political scientist I knew once said to me, "If people really knew why they think the way they do and act the way they do, there would be no need for social science. It is because people cannot judge what is in their own self-interest, cannot know how they got the ideas and beliefs they have, and cannot explain, most times, why they act the way they do, that we need social scientists." Whatever else this book does, it will provide insights that help us understand why human behavior is so curious and enigmatic.

The applications part of the book deals with topics that are important parts of our everyday lives and that reflect culturally significant choices we make involving taste, such as:

yogurt (the average person in America consumes 14 pounds of yogurt in a year), **dogs** (found in 70 million homes in America), **Celine Dion** (a world-famous singer), jokes (which play important roles in our conversations), **facial hair** (why are so many men wearing beards nowadays?), **cruises** (an increasingly important part of tourism), **mysteries** (a popular genre of books) and **smartphones** (owned by 85% of Americans).

You will find that the social, economic, and cultural significance of these topics is of major consequence in America (and many other countries as well), and reveals a great deal about the American character, culture, and taste.

A garment, an automobile, a dish of cooked food, a gesture, a film, a piece of music, an advertising image, a piece of furniture, a newspaper headline—these indeed appear to be heterogeneous objects. What might they have in common? This at least: all are signs. When I walk through the streets—or through life—and encounter these objects I apply to all of them, if need be without realizing it, one and the same activity, which is that of a certain *reading:* modern man, urban man, spends his time reading. He reads, first of all and above all, the images, gestures, behaviors: this car tells me the social status of its owner, this garment tells me quite precisely the degree of its wearer's conformism or eccentricity, this *apéritif* (whiskey, Pernod, or what wine and cassis) reveals my host's lifestyle….All these "readings" are too important in our life, they imply too many social, moral, ideological values, not to attempt to account for them by systematic reflection: it is this reflection which, at least for the moment, we call *semiology.*

Roland Barthes, "The Kitchen of Meaning" (in *The Semiotic Challenge,* 1988).

Language is a system of signs that express ideas, and is therefore comparable to a system of writing, the alphabet of deaf-mutes, symbolic rites, polite formulas, military signals, etc. But it is the most important of all these systems. *A science that studies the life of signs within society* is conceivable; it would be a part of social psychology and consequently of general psychology; I shall call it *semiology* (from the Greek *sēmeîon* "sign"). Semiology would show what constitutes signs, what laws govern them. Since the science does not yet exist, no one can say what it would be; but it has a right to existence, a place staked out in advance

Ferdinand de Saussure, *Course in General Linguistics.* (1966).

Chapter 1

The Semiotics of Taste

Semiotics is the science of signs. A sign can be defined as anything that can stand for something, whether that something exists or not. Semiotics was created, so to speak, by two founding fathers (working separately): a Swiss linguist, Ferdinand de Saussure, and an American philosopher, Charles Sanders Peirce.

What Semiotics Does

A journalist, Maya Pines, gives us a general idea of what semiotics is about. She describes this process in an article as follows ("How They Know What You Really Mean," *San Francisco Chronicle*, Oct 13, 1982):

> Everything we do sends messages about us in a variety of codes, semiologists contend. We are also on the receiving end of innumerable messages encoded in music, gestures, foods, rituals, books, movies, or advertisements. Yet we seldom realize that we have received such messages, and would have trouble explaining the rules under which they operate.

Semiotics helps us interpret the messages we are sent by others and recognize better the messages we send about ourselves to others. People are often unaware of the messages they are sending to others and how they are interpreted, and often make mistakes in interpreting the signs that others are sending us. Semiotics is important since, as Pines explains, "everything we do" involves sending messages about ourselves and interpreting messages others send us.

Figure 1.1: Ferdinand de Saussure

Saussure

Semioticians would explain that these messages are, technically speaking, signs.

Saussure wrote that signs have two components: a sound or object or smell, which he called *a signifier*, and the concepts, ideas, etc. generated by that signifier, which he called a *signified*. The relation between the signifier and signified is arbitrary and can change. The signifier and signified are two sides of the same coin. This relationship is shown below.

Figure 1.2: Signifier/Signified diagram. Berger after Saussure

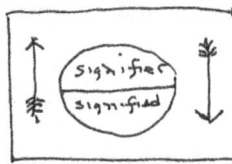

The Basics of Semiotics

Mark Gottdiener, a sociologist, explains the basics of semiotics in his book, *The Theming of America: Dreams, Visions, and Commercial Spaces* (1997:8, 9):

> The basic unit of semiotics is the sign defined conceptually as something that stands for something else, and, more technically, as a spoken or written word, a drawn figure, or a material object unified in the mind with a particular cultural concept. The sign is this unity of word-object, known as a *signifier* with a corresponding, culturally prescribed content or meaning, known as a *signified*. Thus, our minds attach the word "dog," or the drawn figure of a "dog," as a signifier to the idea of a "dog," that is, a domesticated canine species possessing certain behavioral characteristics. If we came from a culture that did not possess dogs in daily life, however unlikely, we would not know what the signifier "dog" means....When dealing with objects that are signifiers of certain concepts, cultural meanings, or ideologies of belief, we can consider them not only as "signs," but *sign vehicles*. Signifying objects carry meanings with them.

In order to interpret signs correctly, we have to know the codes that explain them. This matter is explained by a British semiotician, Daniel Chandler, in his book, *Semiotics: The Basics* (2002:147):

> Since the meaning of a sign depends on the code within which it is situated, codes provide a framework within which signs make sense. Indeed, we cannot grant something the status of a sign if it does not function within a code....The conventions of codes represent a social

dimension in semiotics: a code is a set of practices familiar to users of the medium operating with a broad cultural framework....When studying cultural practices, semioticians treat as signs any objects or actions which have meaning to the members of a cultural group, seeking to identify the rules or conventions of the codes which underlie the production of meaning within that culture.

While you may never have heard the term "semiotics," I would suggest that you've actually been an untutored semiotician all your life. That's because you've spent every moment you've been awake (and if Freud is correct, even when dreaming) involved with making sense of the world.

Peirce, the American founding-father of semiotics (who gave the science its name) argued that everything in the universe is a sign, which means semiotics, understanding how signs generate meaning, and learning how to interpret signs is essential for people to function in the world. If we are always receiving messages (in the form of signs) from others and always sending messages (in the form of signs) to others, semiotics becomes of central significance to us.

Figure 1.3: Facial Expressions.
The author, his wife, and three Brazilians in a photo taken in Rio many years ago

The Semiotics of People Watching

For example, let's consider people watching, which we do all the time. You are sitting in a coffee shop and notice the other people in the shop: what they are wearing, their hairstyles, their hair colors, any jewelry they may have, their body language, their facial expressions, their gestures, and so on. All of these things are signs that we use to figure out something about the people we are watching.

We do the same thing with people in photographs, characters in television commercials, films, and videos. That is, we are always "reading" others for signs they generate and trying to interpret those signs to get a sense of what people are like. I offer now a partial list of some signs people examine when "reading" people.

A Partial List of Signs Involved in Reading People

When we "read" people, here are some of the things we look at (signifiers), often in little more than a momentary glance:

Height: short, medium, tall
Body shape: thin, medium, fat, obese
Body language
Skin color
Race
Ethnicity
Complexion
Gender
Hairstyle
Hair color
Eyebrows
Color of eyes
Eyeglasses style and brand
Ears (do they stick out?)
Ear jewelry
Nose jewelry
Lips (thin, fleshy)
Teeth straightness and color
Chin structure (receding? jutting)?
Size of nose
Shape of the nose (straight? hooked)?
Neck size and length
Facial Expressions
Hat style
Gestures
Hands (rings?)
Fingernails
Handbags, briefcases, backpacks, etc.
Style of clothes
Brands of clothes, smartphones, etc. (when evident)

Color of clothes
Fabric of clothes
Neckwear (if any)
Kind of tie and tie knot
Jackets, coats, outerwear
Kind of shoes
Style of shoes

All of these things are signs that we examine and attempt to interpret in "reading" people or, in semiotic terms, interpreting the messages that people are sending about themselves. We also automatically "read" characters in movies, plays, print advertisements, television commercials, and all other mediated experiences, and every experience we have in which there are people to "read."

We are led to conclude that people often don't recognize that they are always sending messages about themselves or mistakenly think that the messages they are sending about themselves, through the clothes they wear and other matters listed above, will be interpreted correctly. Frequently, people do not interpret the signs that others send about themselves correctly. There is also a problem in people reading, which is that people often lie with signs.

Figure 1.4: Woman with dyed blonde hair

Photo by the author.

Lying With Signs

One problem with interpreting signs is that people can use signs to lie. Thus, a woman with blonde hair who is really a brunette who has dyed her hair is, in a minor way, lying with a sign—her blonde hair. Bald men with wigs are also lying with signs. The point is that we have to be careful when interpreting signs.

Figure 1.5: Umberto Eco

As Umberto Eco, a prominent Italian semiotician, explains in his book, *A Theory of Semiotics* (1976:7):

> Semiotics is concerned with everything that can be taken as a sign. A sign is everything which can be taken as significantly substituting for something else. This something else does not necessarily have to exist or to actually be somewhere at the moment in which a sign stands for it. Thus semiotics is in principle the discipline studying everything which can be used in order to lie. If something cannot be used to tell a lie, conversely, it cannot be used to tell the truth; it cannot be used "to tell" at all.

If signs, Eco points out, can be used to tell the truth, they also must be able to be used to lie. Consider, for example, how people lie about brands with "knock offs."

For semioticians, brands are what Saussure called signifiers that companies use to help establish their identities. The essence of a brand is being different from other brands and from generic products that compete with them. Brands use advertising to establish an image of what they are and what kind of people use their products. Brands are pure connotation.

Saussure said (1915/1965: 120), "in language, there are only differences." From a Saussurean perspective, we can say, "in brands, there are only differences." Brands compete with one another and with generic products or commodities and with "knock-offs." Below is an advertisement for a Rolex "knock-off" on sale for $128.00.

Figure 1.6: https://www.replicamagicwatch.to/

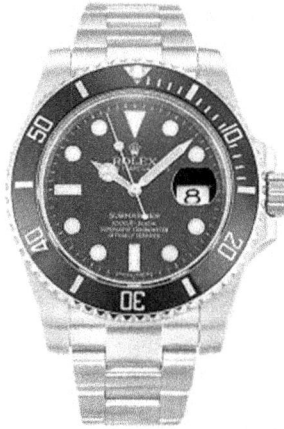

Let's consider "knock-offs," which are imitations of famous brand products, such as handbags, sunglasses, and watches. "Knock-offs" are, technically speaking, from a semiotic perspective, lies. They steal the auras and status that the name brands have. Since many people evaluate others by the brands of products they are wearing, "knock-offs," if they are not recognized for what they are, lead to false assessments about the person with the product. It only makes sense for "knock-offs," like the imitation Rolex watch shown above, to be made only of iconic and expensive brands of products.

People also think about themselves in terms of the brands of products they have and develop what I call "branded selves." People wearing "knock-offs" have to have a different sense of themselves and their status than a person wearing branded products.

We communicate our approval or non-approval of people, products, and other areas where the expression of our emotions is involved, primarily through our facial expressions, though our spoken language, body language, and gestures also are involved in reflecting our attitudes involving taste.

Facial Expressions

Many of our facial expressions are immediate, automatic, and involuntary, such as when we see something or eat something we don't like or, conversely, like a great deal—both emotions are expressions of taste. There are many facial expressions and they vary all over the world, but there are seven universal facial expressions, according to Paul Ekman, a psychologist who has done important research on facial expressions. Ekman, a psychologist, is one of the foremost authorities on facial expression, did extensive research and found that there are seven universal facial expressions and one "neutral" state that doesn't indicate any emotion (Ekman & Sejnowski, 1992). They are as follows, in alphabetical order:

Anger
Determination
Disgust
Fear
Neutral (no expression)
Pouting
Sadness
Surprise

Ekman developed a facial action coding system that explains that there are 43 muscles in the human face, that in different combinations show our emotions. In some cases, an emotion lasts for just a fragment of a second on our faces, what he calls "micro-expressions" which we often aren't aware of showing. Facial expressions reflect cognitive activity like perplexity, concentration, and boredom and reveal truthfulness and lying.

The expressions of most significance as far as the taste of food is concerned are probably disgust, which is what we feel when something tastes terrible, and surprise, when something tastes delicious. These two expressions are extremes, and usually, I would suggest, we often experience expressions in both directions but more moderately.

Facial expressions are signifiers of our preferences involving taste in its myriad forms—whether about people, products, events, foods, whatever. I can recall an experience my wife and I had in India when we were at a restaurant and there were four or five waiters who were standing around us watching our faces intently to see whether we liked the food they had brought us.

Greg Rowland
The Grenade of Taste: Arming the 20th Century Bourgeoisie with an Explosive Abstract Directive.

The notion of Good Taste is fondly recalled by a certain strata of the English bourgeoisie, even if they were born far too late to see it. English "Taste" emerged some time during the nation's imperialist endeavors, and pretty much waned, as a fully weaponized mode of aesthetic choice, once The Beatles emerged and the sun set on the Empire.

Good Taste was entirely the preserve of the haute bourgeoisie, and represented the silent, seething completive fervor that characterizes this social class. The aristocracy had no interest in Good Taste and balked at the merest whiff of modernity. One high Tory once famously remarked of a fellow MP, a young self-made millionaire, that "he was the sort who buys his own furniture." Following the mutable notions of good taste was not for the landed classes. They proffered to wallow in ancient furnishings, handed down by the generation, often falling apart, entirely impractical, not to say unsanitary — but a sore butt and bed mites are a small price to pay for the avoidance of buying one's own furniture.

But for the Middle Classes, Taste was a way of life, an attitude that could be expressed through wise consumption choices in clothing, home furnishings, and cultural choices. But it was their visibility, more than any intrinsic aesthetic appeal, that was the key factor. If one's Good Taste was hidden away, then it lost all its potential to stake a place in the battle against its unspeakable Other, the Poor Taste of the Working Classes, with their maximalist ornaments, heavy wooden dressers, love of the filigree in lace and horribly expressive colored patterns wherever they could place them.

This was the most important aspect of Good Taste, not so much an aesthetic choice, as a constant defensive volley of ideological grenades, ensuring that one's Good Taste declared one's essential difference from not just the Proletariat but one's neighbors, relatives, friends, and associates. The maintenance of visible Good Taste in the home was a restless bunker against status slippage, always threatening to betray the unwary who hadn't considered the cultural work performed by their choice in cutlery, curtains, cushions, and pretty much any domestic item that could accrue value as ordinance in the ongoing war of the Uncovered Home. And what a midfield it represented. You were supposed to reflect your individuality, but not shout too loudly. To offer sufficient evidence of your good taste, but never veer into the clutter of the disorganized and indiscrete working person's living space.

But the spoils were rich for whoever got it right. By force of will, as there were few reliable guides to achieving visible taste, and these could be made redundant by specificities of context or time. Good Taste, like its earthier discursive cousin, Common Sense, tended to be answerable only to itself. A few general avoidance strategies, a negative aesthetics of minimalism, plainness, and perfunctory functionalism might have held sway, but the positive core of what actually codified items of Good Taste remained, necessarily, mysterious. Good Taste, however stressful to maintain, had to be capricious and mysterious, something one born to appreciate and manifest, a sensibility by DNA that was a far subtler inheritance than the oafish upper crust with their dull land and tatty manor houses.

The critical thing for English Good Taste was its provision as a bulwark that licensed criticism of pretty much anyone based on a vague aesthetics bound by reserve, removal, and a delicate lack of presence. On this basis, England found itself able to cheerily disparage almost any nation on earth. But it was Americans that bore the brunt of English bourgeoise distaste. America was a byword for bad taste, commercial excess, for grandiosity, for egregious, shiny, hyper-visibility. Of course, hardly any Americans were aware of this volley of sneers from across the Atlantic, and if they were, perceived it with the wry amusement one might afford an eccentric aunt in full monologue after one too many glasses of sherry wine.

Indeed, a young generation born in wartime adored all things American, and in the case of the Beatles and their cohorts demonstrated no small skill in repackaging American music back to its homeland. And it was upon the backs of the Fab Four, smashing down the barriers of bourgeois Taste and Opportunity, that traditional British notions of a curated social aesthetic began to fracture. The myopic exclusion aesthetics of the previous generations would be replaced by an eclectic hodgepodge of influences —Indian, Japanese, and African artifacts soon adorned middle-class homes. British people even figured out that Sweden did a far more stylish version of minimalism than a version, based on a negative capability default strategy of not getting things wrong.

And it wasn't just a nongeographic scope that transformed good taste — a heightened interest in the past, first in kitschy Victoriana, and later in the 50s, 60s and, eventually, ironic quotations from any decade experienced or imagined in cultural memory, made the identification of a resolute, unified idea of Good Taste virtually impossible. Even the signifiers were now a subject of mockery, "all in the best possible taste," a 1970s catchphrase to indicate something salubrious and downmarket. Typically, just as working people started to afford Good Taste, the middle-classes pulled up the ladder behind them.

But, despite the class conflict, it was British irony, in many ways, that saved us. Finally able to put up whatever rubbish we fancied on our shelves and afford ourselves the distance that the comforts of postmodernity allowed, never again would Good Taste tyrannize the very people that the discourse had originally served so well.

From a commercial perspective, any use of "Taste" on package goods or in ads, beyond the gastronomical, is increasingly rare. Very occasionally, we might see a dainty "collectible" ornament that's been 'tastefully prepared', but signifiers like "curated," "revealed" or "expressed" do the same kind of work, without feeling lodged in the 1950s. And these kinds of pretentious words for making do, if from a somewhat lofty vantage point, point to a signified that includes the idea of manufacture, rather than the abstract miasma of an agreed, but never quite understood, the notion of Good Taste. Essentially, in the UK, an upmarket brand would no more declare itself 'tasteful' than it would 'classy.'

Of course, there is a linguistic constituent who might still regard 'tasteful' and even 'classy' as non-ironic signifiers. Taste, so long a prized weapon of the bourgeoisie, has been released into the hands of the lower orders, just at the cultural moment whereby the whole notion of an agreed 'tastefully' intuitive approach to domestic aesthetics has become something of a sly giggle. So, the middle-classes, through byzantine cultural strategies, still maintain their cultural distance from those beneath them, even if it meant giving up, and then mocking, an idea which once dictated, in vague and capricious ways, a proper way to live through appearance and artifacts.

Greg Rowland was born in 1967, educated at Oxford, and has been a commercial semiotician since 1992. He is based in London and occasionally writes for hilobrow.com. He is a commercial semiotician.

It was a triumph for the interpretative art of psychoanalysis when it succeeded in demonstrating that certain common mental acts of normal people, for which no one had hitherto attempted to put forward a psychological explanation, were to be regarded in the same light as the symptoms of neurotics: that is to say, they had a meaning, which was unknown to the subject but which could easily be discovered by analytic means. . . . A class of material was brought to light which is calculated better than any other to stimulate a belief in the existence of unconscious mental acts even in people to whom the hypothesis of something at once mental and unconscious seems strange and even absurd.

Sigmund Freud (1963). "Psychoanalysis," in Philip Rieff. Ed. *Character and Culture*

We may say that the id comprises the psychic representatives of the drives, the ego consists of those functions which have to do with the individual's relation to his environment, and the superego comprises the moral precepts of our minds as well as our ideal aspirations. The drives, of course, we assume to be present from birth, but the same is certainly not true of interest in or control of the environment on the one hand, nor of any moral sense or aspirations on the other. It is obvious that neither of the latter, that is neither the ego nor the superego, develops till sometime after birth. Freud expressed this fact by assuming that the id comprised the entire psychic apparatus at birth and that the ego and superego were originally parts of the id which differentiated sufficiently in the course of growth to warrant their being considered as separate functional entities.

Charles Brenner. *An Elementary Textbook of Psychoanalysis.* (1974).

You believe that you are informed of all that goes on in your mind if it is of any importance at all, because your consciousness then gives news of it. And if you have heard nothing of any particular thing in your mind you confidently assume that it does not exist there. Indeed, you go so far as to regard "the mind" as coextensive with "consciousness," that is, with what is known to you. . . . Come, let yourself be taught something on this one point. What is in your mind is not identified with what you are conscious of; whether something is going on in your mind and whether you hear of it, are two different things.

Sigmund Freud. "One of the Difficulties of Psychoanalysis." (1910/1963b):

I do not like thee,
Doctor Fell,
The reason why,
I cannot tell;
But this I know and know full well,
I do not like thee, Doctor Fell.
Nursery Rhyme.

Chapter 2

The Psychoanalytic Perspective on Taste

I have already dealt, in passing, with a psychological matter—how semiotics can be used to gain insights into our likes and dislikes from observing our facial expressions when we find ourselves in a situation where taste is a factor. In this chapter, we will consider the human psyche and how it is involved in what we like and don't like—that is, in our tastes.

Figure 2.1: Sigmund Freud

Sigmund Freud's theories about the unconscious are of concern here. He pointed out that the psyche has three components: consciousness, a subconscious (sometimes call the preconscious), and an unconscious. I like to use a simile to describe the human psyche: It is like an iceberg.

A simile is a weak form of metaphor using "is like" or something similar. Metaphor and simile are both based on analogic thinking. Saying that consciousness is *like* an iceberg is thus a simile. Metaphor, I should point out, is a fundamental component of our thinking and is used by people in conversations all the time.

The Unconscious

Figure 2.2: The Iceberg and the Psyche

Conscious
subconscious
unconscious

The tip of the iceberg, which we can see floating above the water, is consciousness—what we are aware of. Just below the waterline, the part of the iceberg we can dimly make out is our subconscious or preconscious. The rest of the iceberg, and by far the greater part (perhaps 85% of it) is our unconscious—material in it that we are unaware of and that gets into it in many ways.

What is important to recognize is that the unconscious shapes our ideas, beliefs, and taste, which means that many of the decisions we make are not based on rationality but on emotions and feelings, and other phenomena in our unconscious.

Gerald Zaltman, a professor of marketing at the Harvard Business School, wrote a book, *How Customers Think: Essential Insights into the Mind of the Market,* which makes an important point. He writes (2003:50):

> Consciousness is crucial in daily life for many obvious reasons. However, an important fact and one of the key principles of this book is the 95-5 split: At least 95 percent of all cognition occurs below awareness in the shadows of the mind while, at most, only 5 percent occurs in high-order consciousness.

He adds, shortly after this passage (2003:55):

> The areas of the human brain that involve choice are activated well before we become consciously aware that we've made a choice. That is, decisions "happen" before they are seemingly "made." In fact, unconscious judgments not only happen before conscious judgments, but they guide them as well.

When we see the terms "choice" and "decisions," we are actually talking, indirectly, about taste, since it is our taste that shapes our choices. Taste, then, is shaped to a considerable degree by forces in our unconscious. In many cases, as Zaltman explains, we have the illusion when we make choices (that are manifestations of our taste) that we are acting rationally.

Freud's Structural Hypothesis

Freud developed a second theory about the psyche as his thought developed. This theory, known as Freud's "structural" hypothesis, suggests that the psyche has three parts: the id, the ego, and the superego. Freud suggested that an unconscious conflict goes on in all people between the id and superego aspects of their personalities.

Freud described the id as "chaos, a cauldron of seething excitement" and said it is characterized by impulse and the desire for gratification. When we think of the id, we should focus on matters such as sexual desire, lust, passion, and desire. Opposed to the id, we find the superego, which represents parental influence, conscience, and restraint. According to Brenner's *An Elementary Textbook of Psychoanalysis* (1974:111-112), the superego can be characterized as follows:

> The approval or disapproval of actions and wishes on the ground of rectitude, 2. critical self-observation, 3. self-punishment, 4. the demand for reparation or repentance of wrong-doing, 5. self-praise or self-love as a reward for virtuous or desirable thoughts and actions. Contrary to the ordinary meaning of "conscience," however, we understand the functions of the superego are often largely or completely unconscious.

The id says, "I want it all and I want it now," and the superego says, "Don't do it or you'll be sorry." The id provides energy and is necessary, but if it is not restrained, we cannot accomplish anything. The superego provides restraint, but if not controlled would overwhelm us all with guilt. These forces operate, generally speaking, at the unconscious level.

Taste, it would seem, manifests itself primarily through the id, which seeks gratifications, based ultimately on the desire for pleasure.

Figure 2.3: Id, Ego and Superego

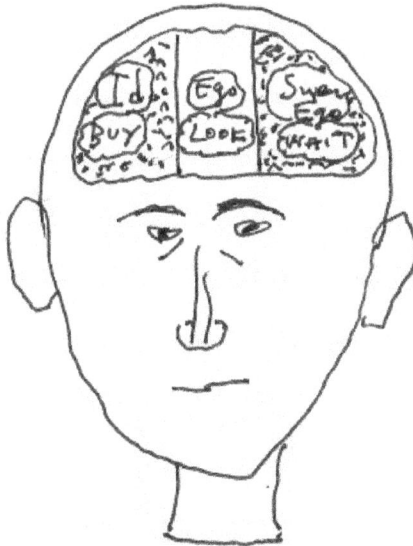

We can use Freud's typology of id, ego, and superego and apply it to our taste for various aspects of popular culture and everyday life, as the chart below shows. What I am suggesting is that there are id, ego, and superego elements in the various book genres we read, magazines we like, films and television shows we watch, and other aspects of popular culture and everyday life. Some blocks have been blank for readers to fill in.

Table 2.1: Popular Culture Preferences and Id/Ego/Superego

TOPIC	ID	EGO	SUPEREGO
Book Genres	Romances, Vampire Novels	Textbooks	Bible, Koran
Magazines	*Playboy*	*National Geographic*	*Today's Christian Living*
Films	*Twilight*	*Murder on the Orient Express*	
Television	Dancing With The Stars	Nova, Nature	"The Blessed Life of Pastor Robert Morris."
Cities	Las Vegas	Boston	Vatican City
Heroes (Fictional)	Don Juan	Sherlock Holmes	Superman, Dick Tracy
Heroines (Fictional)	Emma Bovary	Hermione Granger from *Harry Potter*	Wonder Woman
Toys	Barbie Doll	Science Toys	
Restaurants	Buffets	Ordinary restaurant	Vegetarian
?			
?			

The point is that our ids, egos, and superegos play a role in shaping our taste in popular culture and everyday life. Our preferences are just another way of saying taste or "things we like."

Age and Taste

Age plays an important role in shaping our taste preferences. When we are young children, candy, ice cream, and sweets are of considerable importance to us, but when we are older, we have other preferences. Ironically, for most people, when they are older and can afford as much candy or ice cream as they want, they no longer have a passion for them but do have a taste for alcoholic beverages, gourmet meals, etc.

Figure 2.4: Erik Erikson

Erik Erikson

Erik Erikson, a psychoanalyst, suggests that human beings pass through eight crises as they develop. These stages are shown in the chart below, which I created.

Table 2.2: Erikson's Stages of Development and Crises

Stage	Crisis	Age
Hope	Trust vs. Mistrust	Infancy (under 1 year)
Will	Autonomy vs. Shame	Toddler (1-3 years)
Purpose	Initiative vs. Guilt	Early Childhood (3-6 years)
Competence	Industry vs. Inferiority	Middle Childhood (7-10) years)
Fidelity	Identity vs. Role Confusion	Adolescence (11-19 years)
Love	Intimacy vs. Isolation	Early Adulthood (20-44 years)
Care	Generativity vs. Stagnation	Middle Adulthood (45-64 years)
Wisdom	Ego Integrity vs Despair	Late Adulthood (65 years and beyond)

It is reasonable to assume that as we age, the crises we face differ, the things that we are concerned with differ, and our interests and our taste develop as well.

The great English poet, W. H. Auden, discussed how tastes change in reading in *The Dyer's Hand* published by Faber and Faber (1948:5):

A child's reading is guided by pleasure, but his pleasure is undifferentiated; he cannot distinguish, for example, between aesthetic pleasure and the pleasures of learning or daydreaming. In adolescence, we realize that there are different kinds of pleasure, some of which cannot be enjoyed simultaneously, but we need help from others in defining them. Whether it be a matter of taste in food or taste in literature, the adolescent looks for a mentor in whose authority he can believe. He eats or reads what his mentor recommends and, inevitably, there are occasions when he has to deceive himself a little; he has to pretend that he enjoys olives or War and Peace a little more than he actually does. Between the ages of twenty and forty, we are engaged in the process of discovering who we are, which involves learning the difference between accidental limitations which it is our duty to outgrow, and the necessary limitations of our nature beyond which we cannot trespass with impunity. Few of us can learn this without making mistakes, without trying to become a little more of a universal man than we are permitted to be. It is during this period that a writer can most easily be led astray by another writer or by some ideology. When someone between twenty and forty says, à propos of a work of art, 'I know what I like,' he is really saying 'I have no taste of my own but accept the taste of my cultural milieu', because, between twenty and forty, the surest sign that a man has a genuine taste of his own is that he is uncertain of it. After forty, if we have not lost our authentic selves altogether, pleasure can again become what it was when we were children, the proper guide to what we should read.

Thus, for example, the taste of adolescents may be shaped in part, by what Auden called "mentors" but nowadays by the celebrities and heroes with whom they identify and "influencers" (also who can be thought of as brand advocates) on social media like Facebook or TikTok.

By "identification" we mean the act or process of becoming like something or someone in one or several aspects of thought or behavior. Thus, children, adolescents, and adults often identify with sports heroes or with certain teams and show their identification by wearing a jersey of the team and the number of a star player.

You see this when you watch football games and many people at the games are wearing team jerseys. When we identify with others, we tend to be influenced by their taste preferences.

Figure 2.5: Geoffrey Gorer

Gender and Taste

Geoffrey Gorer is a British anthropologist who applied psychoanalytic theory in his books, such as *The People of Great Russia: A Psychological Study* and *The American People: A Study of National Character.* In his book on American character, he writes (1964:61):

> Market researchers, whose business demands that they be accurate in such matters, reckon that women make more than three-quarters of the retail purchases in the United States. This means there is practically no sphere of design, from men's neckties to automobiles, which does not cater in the first instance to women's taste. And even where women are

not in fact the most important consumers, they are often treated as if they were.

It is reasonable to argue, then, that in America, women's taste plays an important role in our consumption and that taste has been ceded to women in many areas. Gorer contrasts the clinging American mother (who he characterizes as an emotional menace) to the (1964:64) "heavy, domineering father in England and on the Continent," where, as Gorer puts it, (1964:65) "married women in their fifties and sixties are of little importance in the social scene." If Gorer is correct, taste in America is dominated by women.

This may explain why decorating a home can be so difficult for women. As Milton Sapirstein, a psychiatrist, writes in his book *Paradoxes of Everyday Life* (1963:95):

> As the car is a symbol of masculinity, so is the home a symbol of femininity. To a woman, her home is like another, larger body, and all her mysterious impulses find expression within its walls. Her deepest self is implicated in the texture of its draperies, the casual shape of chairs and tables, the dimensions of a bed. As she trudges from shop to shop— examining, comparing, pondering this article or that—her choices are determined by an unconscious image of what she is, or dreads to be.

The home, he adds, is a symbol of exposed femininity. He adds (1963:96):

> The unconscious fear of "exposing not their taste alone, but their inmost selves is what drives a large number of women into the arms of professional decorators."

Sapirstein offers some examples of how unconscious imperatives in women play out: a woman with a strong but unconscious masculine identity would like "starkly modernistic" décor; a woman preoccupied with her bowel movements made her house look like it was a gigantic bathroom; and a woman with bowed legs chose only furniture with no legs.

He summarizes his discussion of women and taste as follows (1963:103):

> Women who are uncertain and anxious about their taste may try to run away from the challenge, taking refuge in a bland admission of incompetence. They may delegate the job to others—mother, husband, or professionals—or resolve their dilemmas by making their homes as indistinguishable as possible from the homes of others in their circle. While this use of accepted formulas may resolve their anxieties, it does not dispose of them altogether. Almost always, it leaves a residue of shame.

Sapirstein is focusing his attention on the anxieties about their taste generated by women decorating their homes, but what he says about women also applies to men and their attitudes about their taste preferences.

We must recognize that the things we buy, and many other choices we make, are shaped in part by our tastes, and are, psychoanalytically speaking, messages that reveal things about us.

I have also suggested in my book, *Media, Myth, and Society,* that ancient myths, in camouflaged forms, play a role in our thinking and behavior. I developed what I describe as a "myth model" that traces these myths through psychoanalytic theory, historical experience, elite culture, popular culture, and everyday life. It is reasonable to suggest that many of our decisions that reflect and shape our tastes have mythic origins.

We can see that from a psychoanalytic perspective, understanding personal taste is an extremely complicated matter shaped by such factors as unconscious imperatives, the relations between the id, ego, and superego elements in our psyche, identifications, challenges we face as we age, and the problematics of gender. It is not too much of a simplification to suggest that gender has moved from the realm of biology to that of taste, and the binary distinction between men and women has been replaced by non-binary attitudes toward gender identity.

I define myth as a sacred narrative that validates cultural beliefs and practices. I offer an example of "myth model" below in my discussion of two myths: Adam and Eve in the Garden, and the Oedipus complex.

The Myth Model

a myth, defined as a sacred narrative that validates cultural beliefs and practices

psychoanalytic reflections of the myth (found in psychoanalytic theory)

historical manifestations of that myth (found in actions of men and women)

the myth in elite culture (found in operas, plays, ballets, serious novels, etc.)

the myth in mass-mediated or popular culture (in comic books, television shows, romance novels, etc.)

the myth in everyday life (typical experiences from waking up to going to sleep)

My idea for developing a model came from reading Mircea Eliade, who explained in *The Sacred and The Profane* that many things that people do in contemporary society are actually camouflaged or modernized versions of ancient myths and legends. As Eliade writes: (1961:204-205):

The modern man who feels and claims that he is nonreligious still retains a large stock of camouflaged myths and degenerated rituals. As we remarked earlier, the festivities that go with the New Year or with taking up residence in a new house, though laicized, still exhibit the structure of a ritual of renewal. The same phenomenon is observable in the merrymaking that accompanies a marriage or a social advancement, and so on. A whole volume could well be written on the myths of modern man, on the mythologies camouflaged in the plays that he enjoys, in the books that he reads. The cinema, that "dream factory," takes over and employs countless mythological motifs—the fight between hero and monster, initiatory combats and ordeals, paradigmatic figures (the maiden, the hero, the paradisal landscape, hell, and so on). Even reading includes a mythological function, not only because it replaces the recitation of myths in archaic societies and the oral literature that still lives in the rural communities of Europe, but particularly because, through reading, the modern man succeeds in obtaining an "escape from time" comparable to the "emergence from time" effected by myths.

Here are two examples of myths and the answers they generate when they are run through the myth model.

Table 2.3: The Myth Model

Myth/Sacred Story	Adam in the Garden of Eden. Theme of natural innocence.	Oedipus Myth. Theme of son unknowingly killing father and marrying mother.
Psychoanalytic manifestation.	Repression? Suppression?	Oedipus complex. Love of child for parent of opposite gender.
Historical Experience	Puritans come to U.S.A. to escape corrupt European civilization. Binary view of gender.	Revolutions: American, French, Arab awakenings
Elite Culture	American Adam figure in American novels. Henry James' *The American*	Sophocles, *Oedipus Rex* Shakespeare, *Hamlet*
Popular Culture	Westerns…restore natural innocence to Virgin Land. *Shane.*	Jack the Giant Killer James Bond stories *King Kong*
Everyday Life	Escape from city and move to suburbs so kids can play on grass (and smoke grass).	Oedipus period in little children

Figure 2.6: Judith Butler

Gender, Judith Butler argues in her book, *Gender Trouble*, is best seen as a performance and is socially constructed. It is not a binary matter of being either male or female. So gender, we may say, is based on taste and not on biology.

In the first chapter of *Gender Trouble*, titled "Subjects of Sex/Gender/Desire," Butler writes about the relationship that exists between sex and gender (1999:9,10):

> Originally intended to dispute the biology-is-destiny formulation, the distinction between sex and gender serves the argument that whatever biological intractability sex appears to have, gender is culturally constructed: hence, gender is neither the casual result of sex nor as seemingly fixed as sex....If gender is the cultural meanings that the sexed body assumes, then gender cannot be said to follow from a sex in any one way. Taken to its logical limit, the sex/gender distinction suggests a radical discontinuity between sexed bodies and culturally constructed genders. Assuming for the moment the stability of binary sex, it does not follow that the construction of "men" will accrue exclusively to the bodies of males or that "women" will interpret only female bodies. Further, even if the sexes appear to be unproblematically binary in their morphology and constitution (which will become a question), there is no reason to assume that genders ought also to remain at two.

This means that for Butler, gender is not "fixed" at birth, but is socially constructed. This suggests that one can change one's gender since it does not automatically follow from one's sex "in any way." Her book is an attempt to disrupt the conventional ways that people feel about gender The LGBTIQ+ movement is a testimonial to that matter.

Psychology and Psychoanalysis

We can distinguish between psychology and psychoanalysis. According to the American Psychology Association, psychology is the scientific study of mind and behavior. From this perspective, psychoanalysis is a branch of psychology, a social science with immense scope, studying matters such as attention, brain functioning, cognition, intelligence, memory, motivation, unconscious processes, and personality. As might be expected, there are many schools of psychology, from psychoanalysts who focus on the psyche and the unconscious, experimental psychologists, behaviorists, such as B. F. Skinner, who have no interest in the psyche, and so on.

Psychology Today offers a useful definition of psychoanalysis:

> Psychoanalysis refers both to a theory of how the mind works and a treatment modality. In recent years, both have yielded to more research-driven approaches, but psychoanalysis is still a thriving field and deals with subjective experience in ways that other therapies sometimes do not.

> Belief in such hallmarks of Freudian thinking as the primacy of the unconscious fantasy, sexual desires (libido, penis envy, Oedipal complex), and dreams has wavered. But Freud also identified such basic mental maneuvers as transference, projection, and defensiveness, and demonstrated how they distort functioning. As a treatment based on extended self-exploration, psychoanalysis has evolved beyond the silent-shrink stereotype.

> https://www.psychologytoday.com/us/basics/psychoanalysis

We must recognize that psychoanalytic theory is also used by literary critics analyzing works of fiction, literary theorists, biographers, political scientists, sociologists, anthropologists, economists, and scholars in many disciplines, and is not confined to therapeutic interventions.

With these distinctions between psychology and psychoanalysis in mind, we can now consider Bourdieu's ideas about psychology and its relation to sociology. He argues in his book, *Sociology in Question*, that the distinction between sociology and psychology is incorrect. As he explains (1993:15):

> Social science has always stumbled on the problem of the individual and society. In reality, the divisions of social science into psychology, social psychology and sociology were, in my view, constituted around an initial error of definition. The self-evidence of biological individuation prevents people from seeing that society exists in two separable forms: on the one hand, institutions that may take the form of physical beings,

monuments, books, instruments, etc., and, on the other, acquired dispositions, the durable ways of being or doing that are incorporated in bodies (and which I call *habitus*)...

Contrary to the common preconception that associates sociology with the collective, it has to be pointed out that the collective is deposited *in each individual* in the form of durable dispositions, such as mental structures. For example, in *Distinction*, I try to establish empirically the relationship between the social classes and the incorporated systems of classification that are produced in collective history and acquired in individual history—such as those implemented by taste (the oppositions heavy/light, hot/cold, brilliant/dull, etc.).

Bourdieu plays down the distinction between the sociological and psychological, pointing out that the social is found in the individual, which forms the basis of what we might describe as a social psychological perspective on taste. Emile Durkheim, the great French sociologist, said the same thing. Individuals are in society and society is in individuals, which means both psychology and sociology have to be considered with thinking about human behavior.

In his book, *Sociology in Question*, Bourdieu asserts that people's social class can be infallibly identified based on their preferred music styles or the radio station they prefer. With this in mind, let's consider some psychological studies of musical taste. It turns out, research suggests, that musical taste is not only a signifier of one's class but also of one's personality.

Taste in Music: Psychological Studies

There is considerable evidence that taste in music reflects human personality traits, as the following discussion demonstrates:

In 2016, University of Cambridge music psychologist David Greenberg performed a study with his colleagues called "The Song Is You," aimed at evaluating how the main three dimensions of music, "arousal" (the energy level of music), "valence" (the spectrum from sad to happy emotions in music) and "depth" (the amount of sophistication and emotional depth in music), are linked to the Big Five personality traits: openness, conscientiousness, extraversion, agreeableness, and neuroticism.

Their results are what one might generally expect — self-assured people were more likely to enjoy positive music, while those who seek excitement prefer high arousal music. Greenberg says that those who were defined as open-minded had not only a more general preference for music overall, but were also more open to music that spanned genres or might be defined as "genre-fluid."

16 Personalities, an online Myers-Briggs test that has been taken by more than 388 million people so far, has even found strong links between music taste and the 16 different personality types they identified. "Analyst" type personalities, they found, tend to be those that "are most often respected for the sheer technical expertise at work as much as for the more emotional qualities of these songs," such as rock, classical, and jazz. They also tend to be the heaviest users of headphones.... "The idea that music is solely entertainment, or even just a pure aesthetic experience, is very misguided," Greenberg explains. "Music is a form of language. It's a part of human evolution, and it's deeply embedded into our brains."

https://thehill.com/changing-america/enrichment/arts-culture/546777 -science-now-says-you-can-judge-people-by-their-taste.

What we learn from this material is that our taste in music indicates a great deal about our personalities, and as Bourdieu explained, our social class and what he would describe as our cultural capital.

Sociology is the study of human social relationships and institutions. Sociology's subject matter is diverse, ranging from crime to religion, from the family to the state, from the divisions of race and social class to the shared beliefs of a common culture, and from social stability to radical change in whole societies. Unifying the study of these diverse subjects of study is sociology's purpose of understanding how human action and consciousness both shape and are shaped by surrounding cultural and social structures.

Sociology is an exciting and illuminating field of study that analyzes and explains important matters in our personal lives, our communities, and the world. At the personal level, sociology investigates the social causes and consequences of such things as romantic love, racial and gender identity, family conflict, deviant behavior, aging, and religious faith. At the societal level, sociology examines and explains matters like crime and law, poverty and wealth, prejudice and discrimination, schools and education, business firms, urban community, and social movements. At the global level, sociology studies such phenomena as population growth and migration, war and peace, and economic development.

Sociologists emphasize the careful gathering and analysis of evidence about social life to develop and enrich our understanding of key social processes. The research methods sociologists use are varied. Sociologists observe the everyday life of groups, conduct large-scale surveys, interpret historical documents, analyze census data, study videotaped interactions, interview participants of groups, and conduct laboratory experiments. The research methods and theories of sociology yield powerful insights into the social processes shaping human lives and social problems and prospects in the contemporary world. By better understanding those social processes, we also come to understand more clearly the forces shaping the personal experiences and outcomes of our own lives. The ability to see and understand this connection between broad social forces and personal experiences — what C. Wright Mills called "the sociological imagination" — is extremely valuable academic preparation for living effective and rewarding personal and professional lives in a changing and complex society.

https://sociology.unc.edu/undergraduate-program/sociology-major/what-is-sociology/

Chapter 3

The Sociology of Taste

Human beings are social animals, and sociology is the study of how groups and institutions function, and the various arrangements we make to facilitate socialization so we can live with others. The term "sociology" is used very broadly here to represent the social sciences in general.

The Individual and Society

Figure 3.1: Emile Durkheim

Emile Durkheim, the father of French sociology, explained that the relationships between an individual and society are complicated. In his classic study, The *Elementary Forms of the Religious Life*, Durkheim (1915/1965:29) writes about this relationship:

> There are two beings in him: an individual being which has its foundation in the organism and the circle of whose activities is therefore strictly limited, and a social being which represents the highest reality in the intellectual and moral order that we can know by observation—I mean society. This duality of our nature has as its consequence in the practical order, the irreducibility of a moral ideal to a utilitarian motive, and in the order of thought, the irreducibility of reason to individual experience. In so far as he belongs to society, the individual transcends himself, both when he thinks and when he acts.

So, we are, in a sense, double: we are in society, as individuals, and society is in us, which means that social institutions, mores, and codes affect us whether or not we recognize this.

The country where we grow up, what our families are like (especially in terms of socio-economic class), what languages we speak, our religion, our race, and many other similar demographic matters play a role in our thinking and behavior. And our taste preferences.

Figure 3.2: Clotaire Rapaille

Clotaire Rapaille

Clotaire Rapaille and Codes

A French psychoanalyst and marketer, Clotaire Rapaille, wrote a book that deals with the differences among countries on various topics related to taste. In his book, *The Culture Code: An Ingenious Way to Understand Why People Around the World Buy and Live as They Do*, he points out that nations all imprint different codes into children, which shape their behavior, thinking, and taste, in their adult lives. As Rapaille (2006:21) explains:

> I like to say that you never get a second chance to have a first experience. Most of us imprint the meanings of the things most central to our lives by the age of seven. This is because emotion is the central force for children under the age of seven (if you need proof of this watch how often a young child's emotional state changes in a single hour), while after this, they are going by logic (again, try arguing with a nine-year-old). Most people are exposed to only one culture before the age of seven.

Rapaille suggests that three kinds of "unconscious" shape our behavior:

A **Freudian individual unconscious** (which was dealt with earlier),

A **Jungian collective unconscious** (which will be ignored), and

A **cultural unconscious**, which represents the codes imprinted on us that shape our behavior, which is of most interest to us.

His book confirms what we have always suspected is true—that, despite our common humanity, people around the world are really different. Rapaille suggests that imprints are coded and if we wish to shape people's behavior, we have to find the proper code. He offers an interesting example. The French code for cheese is ALIVE, while the American code for cheese is DEAD. Thus, the French store cheese at room temperature in containers called "cloches," while the Americans store it in "morgues" also known as refrigerators.

The Culture Code deals with codes for things in different countries and is, in effect, a study of taste, though Rapaille doesn't use the term when he discusses what his research has discovered about the cultural codes in the countries he writes about. I would argue that if you scratch beneath the surface of the codes Rapaille discusses, you find taste.

He concludes his book with a passage titled "Your Prescription is Ready" that reads as follows (2006:198-199):

> The Culture Code offers the benefits of great new freedom gained from understanding why you act the way you do. It gives a new set of glasses with which you can see the world in a new way. We are all individuals, and each of us has a complex set of motivations, inspirations, and guiding principles—a personal Code, if you will. However, seeing how we think *as a culture,* how we behave as a group in predictable patterns based on the survival kit we received at birth as Americans, or English, or French, enables us to navigate our world with a vision we've heretofore lacked.

It is our culture and the way it is, or its manifestation as a particular and distinctive national character with national codes, that is of particular concern in this chapter.

Geoffrey Gorer, a controversial British anthropologist whose work I discussed earlier, offers us a perspective on national character in his book, *The People of Great Russia: A Psychological Study.* He writes, in the Introduction to the book, about the way cultures maintain themselves (1961: xxxix):

> If we accept the fact that all the peoples of the world are human, with the same physiology and the same psychological potentialities, whatever their present level of technological development, system of values, or political organization, and that all human beings are organized into societies with distinctive cultures, then all human beings and human societies can be studied, at least potentially, by scientific techniques which have been developed to these ends. Of these scientific techniques, social anthropology and whole-person psychology (including depth psychology and developmental data of ethology) are the most appropriate.

> Psychology has shown that in the life of any individual, the process of learning is cumulative, so that early learning influences later learning; social anthropology has shown that culture is continuous over more

than one generation, that the people who die are replaced by new members who have learned, by both conscious and unconscious processes, the values and customs appropriate to their culture and their position in it, or, in other words, their individual variation of the national character.

What we learn from Rapaille and Gorer is that there are national codes that can also be described as a national character found in countries, and these phenomena, imprinted upon us when we are children, play an important role in shaping many aspects of our lives, including our taste.

Figure 3.3: Mary Douglas

Grid-Group Theory and Preferences

Mary Douglas, an English social anthropologist, developed what she called grid-group theory. Her theory is described in Michael Thompson, Richard Ellis, and Aaron Wildavsky's *Cultural Theory* (1990:5):

> [Douglas] argues that the variability of an individual's involvement in social life can be adequately captured by two dimensions of sociality: group and grid. Group refers to the extent to which an individual is incorporated into bounded units. The greater the incorporation, the more individual choice is subject to group determination. Grid denotes the degree to which an individual's life is circumscribed by externally imposed prescriptions. The more binding and extensive the scope of prescriptions, the less of life is open to individual negotiation.

Wildavsky explained in his article, "Conditions for a Pluralist Democracy, or Cultural Pluralism Means More Than One Political Culture in a Country (1982:7):

> What matters to people is how they should live with other people. The great questions of social life are "Who am I?" (To what kind of a group do I belong?) and "What should I do?" (Are there many or few prescriptions

I am expected to obey?). Groups are strong or weak according to whether they have boundaries separating them from others. Decisions are taken either for the group as a whole (strong boundaries) or for individuals or families (weak boundaries). Prescriptions are few or many, indicating the individual internalizes a large or a small number of behavioral norms to which he or she is bound. By combining boundaries with prescriptions . . . the most general answers to the questions of social life can be combined to form four different political cultures.

What Wildavsky defined as political cultures are, for Douglas, "lifestyles." These "lifestyles" are based on whether the group boundaries are strong or weak and whether the number of rules and prescriptions are many or few for the people in each "lifestyle." This yields four "lifestyles" which can be seen from the following figure:

Table 3.1: The Four Lifestyles

Lifestyle	Group Boundaries	Rules and Prescriptions
Fatalists	Weak	Numerous
Individualists	Weak	Few
Egalitarians	Strong	Few
Elitists	Strong	Numerous

Wildavsky described these "lifestyles" as follows (cited in A.A. Berger, 1990:6):

Strong groups with numerous prescriptions that vary with social roles combine to form hierarchical collectivism [also known as elitists]. Strong groups whose members follow few prescriptions form an egalitarian culture, a shared life of voluntary consent, without coercion or inequality. Competitive individualism joins few prescriptions with weak boundaries, thereby encouraging ever new combinations. When groups are weak and prescriptions strong, so that decisions are made for them by people on the outside, the controlled culture is fatalistic.

What is important for us to recognize is that membership in a particular lifestyle plays an important role in determining our taste preferences in many areas. Douglas wrote an article, "In Defence of Shopping," which is found in P. Falk and C. Campbell (Eds.), *The Shopping Experience.* As she explains (1997:19):

None of these four lifestyles (individualist, hierarchical, enclavist, isolated), fatalist, is new to students of consumer behavior. What may be new and unacceptable is the point that these are the only four distinctive lifestyles to be taken into account, and the other point, that each is set up in competition with the others. Mutual hostility is the force that accounts for their stability.

These "lifestyles" are important because, Douglas writes, they shape our choices in many areas. It is our cultural alignments—that is, our membership in one of the "lifestyles" that are the strongest predictors of our consumer preferences, which involves rejecting the kinds of consumer choices made by members of other "lifestyles." She writes (1997:17):

> We have to make a radical shift away from thinking about consumption as a manifestation of individual choices. Culture itself is the result of a myriad of individual choices, not primarily between commodities but between kinds of relationships. The basic choice a rational individual has to make is the choice about what kind of society to live in. According to that choice, the rest follows. Artefacts are selected to demonstrate that choice. Food is eaten, clothes are worn, cinema, books, music, holidays, all the rest are choices that conform with the initial choice for a form of society.

When Douglas uses the word "society" she is referring to "lifestyles." She argues that it is our lifestyle and not individual taste and preferences that shape our decision-making and consumer behavior. What seems to be individual taste, Douglas suggests, is based on unconscious or unrecognized imperatives located in the lifestyle to which people belong. Shopping, she explains, is agonistic—and is based on a struggle to define what we are not, which means rejecting the kinds of choices made by members of other "lifestyles."

What is more interesting, according to her theory, is how cultural biases shape our behavior. "Shopping," she writes, "is agonistic—a struggle not to define what one is, but what one is not," which means that shopping is, ultimately, an act of cultural defiance. Once we choose or find ourselves in a "lifestyle," the rest follows: what we eat, what we wear, what films we choose to see, and so on, which means that, in essence, our taste in these and other areas is more or less determined.

Uses and Gratifications and Taste

Uses and gratifications theory deals with the ways people use media and the gratifications media offer to people. Katz, Blumler, and Gurevitch (1979:215) mention some early works on the subject:

> Herzog (1942) on quiz programs and the gratifications derived from listening to soap operas; Suchman (1942) on the motives for getting interested in serious music on the radio; Wolfe and Fiske (1949) on the development of children's interest in comics; Berelson (1949) on the functions of newspaper reading; and so on. Each of these investigations came up with a list of functions served either by some specific contents or by the medium in question: to match one's wits against others, to get

information or advice for daily living, to provide a framework for one's day, to prepare oneself culturally for the demands of upward mobility, or to be reassured about the dignity and usefulness of one's role.

You may think that soap operas are mindless or that situation comedies are silly, but the functions these programs—and other kinds of media—perform for people may sometimes be quite important. Here is a list of some of the more important uses and gratifications provided by the media:

1. To be amused
2. To see authority figures exalted or deflated
3. To experience the beautiful
4. To share experiences with others
5. To satisfy curiosity and be informed
6. To identify with the deity and the divine plan
7. To find distraction and diversion
8. To experience empathy
9. To experience, in a guilt-free situation, extreme emotions
10. To find models to imitate
11. To gain identity
12. To gain information about the world
13. To reinforce belief in justice
14. To reinforce belief in romantic love
15. To reinforce belief in magic, the marvelous, and the miraculous
16. To see others make mistakes
17. To see order imposed on the world
18. To participate vicariously in history.

This theory about uses and gratifications offers us an inventory of factors involving taste. If something is useful to us, if something provides gratifications, there is reason to assume it is something we like, and thus, is an indirect manifestation of choice. Many of the choices we make in consumption and other areas of life involve finding ways to avoid cognitive dissonance and ways to reinforce the beliefs and values we have. Both phenomena may be at work in determining what we like and don't like, which can be seen as a form or aspect of taste.

Claritas and Taste

Claritas is a marketing research company (among other things) that has developed a typology of sixty-eight categories of consumers found in the United States who live within certain ZIP codes since, as Claritas puts it, "birds of a feather flock together." By this, they mean that people in certain categories often live near one another and share ZIP codes.

Claritas gives each category a jazzy name and a number that shows where they exist in the American consumer culture pecking order. The lower one's number, generally speaking, the more income and status one has. Below, are the top ten highest categories and the top ten lowest categories.

Highest Categories	Lowest Categories
01: Upper-Crust	58: Golden Ponds
02: Networked Neighbors	59: New Melting Pot
03: Movers & Shakers	60. Small-Town Collegiate
04: Young Digerati	61: Second City Generations
05: Country Squires	62: Crossroad Villager
06: Winner's Circle	63: Low-Rise Living
07: Money & Brains	64: Family Thrifts
08: Gray Power	65: Young & Rustic
09: Big Fish, Small Pond	66. New Beginnings
10: Executive Suites	67: Park Bench Seniors
11: Fast-Track Families	68: Bedrock America

These terms are more or less self-evident, but if you wish more information about Claritas, go to its website and check for the clusters in your ZIP code. Claritas provides information about each of these clusters. Not everyone in a ZIP code "belongs," as Claritas sees things, because, for example, some people in my ZIP code are grandfathered in, and purchased their homes before the area became so expensive.

In theory, Claritas provides what we might describe as distinctive "taste" groups, which makes it possible for advertising agencies to target the various groups more precisely. People who fit under the "family thrifts" category are probably not interested in advertisements for companies that sell stocks and bonds. What this suggests is that socio-economic status plays a role in determining our tastes and the possibilities we might have to satisfy them. Some marketing agencies use things like magazine choices to gauge consumer taste while others use consumer media preferences, surveys, and whatever other means they can find to determine what people like and why they like what they like.

Figure 3.4: Herbert Gans

Herbert Gans

Herbert Gans and Taste Cultures

Herbert Gans, a sociologist who was interested in media and popular culture, suggests that there are five "taste cultures" in the United States. As Gans (1974) writes in his book, *Popular Culture and High Culture: An Evaluation of Taste* (1974:x):

> I suggest that America is actually made up of a number of taste cultures, each with its own art, literature, music, and so forth, which differ mainly in that they express different aesthetic standards....The underlying assumption of this analysis is that all taste cultures are of equal worth....Because taste cultures reflect the class and particular education attributes of their publics, low culture is as valid for poorly educated Americans as high culture is for well-educated ones, even if the higher cultures are, in the abstract, better or more comprehensive than the lower cultures.

The chart below lists each of the five taste cultures and offers examples of their pop culture and cultural preferences. We must keep in mind that Gans published his book in 1974, so many of the choices he mentions are time bound and some magazines he mentions are no longer being published. The following table is based on the discussions of taste in his book.

Table 3.2: Gans on Taste Culture Preferences in the Seventies

High Culture	Upper-Middle	Lower-Middle	Low Culture	Quasi-Folk
Formalistic Modern Music	Time, Newsweek	*Life*	Westerns	Comic Books
Primitive Art	Biographies of Achievers	*Look*	*I Love Lucy*	Old Westerns
Abstract Expressionism	Feminist Books	*Reader's Digest*	*The Lawrence Welk Show*	Mexican action films
Finnegan's Wake by James Joyce	*The New Yorker*	*Saturday Evening Post*	*Beverly Hillbillies*	Mexican soap operas
Serious Essays	*Harper's*	*Novels by Harold Robbins*	*Maude*	Church and Street Festivals
	Vogue	*Bonanza*	*Ed Sullivan Show*	Young Graffiti Artists
	Playboy	*All in the Family*	Tabloids	

Gans defended the media and popular culture preferences of the members of each of his taste cultures and suggested that we shouldn't look down on any of their choices, because each text was appropriate for the people who belonged in each taste culture. Gans devotes a few pages in his book to youth cultures, Black cultures, and ethnic cultures but doesn't go into detail about any of them because he believes they are only (1974:94) "temporary offshoots from the taste cultures described previously."

We might wonder about the kind of texts members of each of Gans's taste cultures would like in contemporary, postmodern America. We can also wonder whether the Gans typology is the best way to characterize the American media public, or any media public, for that matter. Are there more than five "taste cultures" in the United States or fewer, as Grid-Group theorists would suggest?

His book is useful to us because he provides specific examples reflecting the taste preferences—as he sees things—of different classes or groupings of Americans. We must recognize that people from high culture and upper-middle culture may also enjoy texts from lower cultures in his typology and it is possible that people in lower taste cultures might enjoy some items from high culture (often also known as "elite" culture), though I can't imagine many people from a low taste culture would find James Joyce's *Finnegan's Wake* interesting or even readable.

Figure 3.5: James Joyce

It is also doubtful whether many people from high or elite culture actually have read *Finnegan's Wake*, though they may have read his *Ulysses*.

In their article, "Taste Regimes and Market-Mediated Practice," Zeynep Arsel and Jonathan Bean offer a useful perspective and summary of sociological perspectives on taste, which suggests that neither Bourdieu nor postmodernist theories of taste are adequate to explain taste. This article appeared in the *Journal of Consumer Research* (Vol. 39, February 2013:899-917):

> Central to literature in consumer research and to sociological accounts of taste is a Bourdieuian formulation of class conditioned habitus. In Bourdieu's terms, "habitus" is seen to structure the embodied attitudes, preferences, and habits that naturalize systems of distinction through everyday practice (Bourdieu 1990). Habitus corresponds with strict social class hierarchies, because it inscribes "schemes of perception, thought and action, [which] tend to guarantee the 'correctness' of practices and their constancy over time, more reliably than all formal rules and explicit norms." Thus, taste is seen as a resource for, and a means of, making social distinction through everyday practice. Critiques of

Bourdieuian explanations of taste argue that a rigid conceptualization of social hierarchy overplays the hegemony of a dominant culture and neglects nuanced systems of social distinctions... Furthermore, recent research theorizes people as cultural omnivores who consume a mix of products and services across categories of high, middle, and low.

They argue that in postmodern societies, consumers must be understood as liberated subjects who can choose from an enormous number of resources. Their behavior is shaped by socially accepted cultural practices.

In his book, *You May Also Like: Taste in an Age of Endless Choice,* Tom Vanderbilt offers some insights into Bourdieu's thinking. Vanderbilt discusses oppositions in Bourdieu's thought and writes (2017:197-198):

Bourdieu insisted these "oppositions" were found not only in cultural practices but in more mundane things like "eating habits." He wanted to tear down the old Kantian divide between "aesthetic consumption"—the art we liked—and "the world of ordinary consumption": the baser pleasures of what we ate and bought. He saw taste at work everywhere. "Taste is the basis of all that one has—people and things—and all that one is for others," wrote Bourdieu. "The science of taste has to abolish the sacred frontier which makes legitimate culture a separate universe, in order to discover the intelligible relations which unite apparently incommensurable 'choices,' such as preferences in music and food, painting and sport, literature and hairstyle.

With these insights from sociologists in mind, we turn to the next perspective on taste, what we can describe as a Marxist approach to taste.

Applied to any aspect of culture, Marxist method seeks to explicate the manifest and latent or coded reflections of modes of material production, ideological values, class relations, and structures of social power—racial or sexual as well as politico-economic—or the state of consciousness of people in a precise historical or socio-economic situation . . . The Marxist method, recently in varying degrees of combination with structuralism and semiology, has provided an incisive analytic tool for studying the political signification in every facet of contemporary culture, including popular entertainment in TV and films, music, mass-circulation books, newspaper and magazine features, comics, fashion, tourism, sports, and games, as well as such acculturating institutions as education, religion, the family and child-rearing, social and sexual relations between men and women—all the patterns of work, play, and other customs of everyday life....The most frequent theme in Marxist cultural criticism is the way the prevalent mode of production and the ideology of the ruling class in any society dominate every phase of culture, and at present, the way capitalist production and ideology dominate American culture, along with that of the rest of the world that American business and culture have colonized. This domination is perpetuated both through overt propaganda in political rhetoric, news reporting, advertising, and public relations and through the often unconscious absorption of capitalistic values by creators and consumers in all the above aspects of the culture of everyday life.

Donald Lazere. *College English.* 1977.

Chapter 4
Marxism and Taste

Marxism is a very complicated subject to deal with because there are many varieties of Marxists. There are Marxist economists, Marxist sociologists, Marxist semioticians, Marxist literary critics, Marxist historians, and so on. Roland Barthes, one of the most prominent semioticians, was also a Marxist, and his book, *Mythologies* is a study of French popular culture, French material culture, and French taste from a Marxist and semiotic perspective.

Figure 4.1: Karl Marx

Marxist Theories

As the Lazere material in the epigraph points out, Marxist theories have been used as a powerful means of critiquing capitalist society and the way the ruling classes in capitalist societies dominate the thinking of the proletariat—the Marxist term for ordinary people.

In Marx's *Selected Writings in Sociology and Social Philosophy,* he discusses the relationship that exists between society and consciousness (1964:51):

In the social production which men carry on, they enter into definite relations that are indispensable and independent of their will; these relations of production correspond to a definite stage of development of their material powers of production. The totality of these relations of production constitutes the economic structure of society—the real foundation on which legal and political superstructures arise and to which definite forms of social consciousness correspond. The mode of production of material life determines the general character of the social, political, and spiritual processes of life. It is not the consciousness of men that determines their being, but, on the contrary, their social being determines their consciousness.

It is the mode of production (economic relationships), then, that is the base or the "determinant element" in our thoughts, and it is people's social being that determines their consciousness, not the other way around. Everything is shaped (but not determined) ultimately by the economic system found in a society. The economic system, in subtle ways, affects the ideas that individuals have, ideas that help to determine the kinds of arrangements people will make with one another, the institutions they will establish, and so on.

Marx on False Consciousness

Marx's notion of false consciousness explains how the ruling classes maintain their dominance over other classes found in a society. He writes in his *Selected Writings in Sociology and Social Philosophy* (1964:78):

> The ideas of the ruling class are, in every age, the ruling ideas: i.e., the class which is the dominant material force in society is at the same time its dominant intellectual force. The class which has the means of material production at its disposal, has control at the same time over the means of mental production, so that in consequence the ideas of those who lack the means of mental production are, in general, subject to it. The dominant ideas are nothing more than the ideal expression of the dominant material relationships, the dominant material relationships grasped as ideas, and thus of the relationships which make one class the ruling one; they are consequently the ideas of its dominance. The individuals composing the ruling class possess, among other things, consciousness, and therefore think. Insofar, therefore, as they rule as a class and determine the whole extent of an epoch, it is self-evident that they do this in their whole range and thus, among other things, rule also as thinkers, as producers of ideas, and regulate the production and distribution of the ideas of their age. Consequently, their ideas are the ruling ideas of their age.

If we substitute "taste" for "ideas," we can see how Marxist theory might explain people's tastes. If ideas are socially constructed and shaped, then so is taste. This is a difficult idea for many people to accept because they believe their taste is personal and tied to their life experiences and personalities, but as was explained in the sociology chapter, there is good reason to believe that taste is connected to one's social being or one's "lifestyle" as the grid-group theorists argue. We now believe that something as fundamental as gender is socially constructed, so taste in gender is but one example of how society shapes taste in many areas of life, especially when it comes to consumer cultures.

The Problem of Alienation

Marxists argue that capitalism is good at producing goods and convincing people to focus much of their energy on consumption, as a means of dealing with the alienation that is a product of capitalism. Erich Fromm, a leading interpreter of Marx, argues that alienation is the core of Marx's theories. As he explains in *Beyond the Chains of Illusion: My Encounter with Marx and Freud* (1962:43-44):

> The concept of alienation has become increasingly the focus of the discussion of Marx's ideas in England, France, Germany, and the U.S.A. . . . The majority of those involved in this debate . . . take a position that alienation and the task of overcoming it is the center of Marx's socialist humanism and the aim of socialism; furthermore that there is a complete continuity between the young and the mature Marx, in spite of changes in terminology and emphasis.

Not all Marxists would agree with Fromm about the continuity between the young and the mature Marx, but would agree with Fromm about alienation being central to understanding Marx.

Figure 4.2: Fritz Pappenheim

Fritz Pappenheim

Fritz Pappenheim, a German Marxist, has written a book, *The Alienation of Modern Man*, that deals with alienation in many areas. In his introduction, he offers an important insight into the role of alienation in our lives (1967:13-14):

> The individual's alienation from everything which has no bearing on the pursuit of his interests does not necessarily enter into his consciousness; nor does he always become aware of the estrangement from his own self or feel it as a disquieting experience. As a result of his detachment, the alienated man is often able to achieve great successes. These, as long as they continue, engender a certain numbness, which makes it hard for him to realize his own estrangement. Only in times of crisis does he start to sense it.

One might argue, from a Marxist perspective, that not only are we estranged from our own selves, we are also estranged from our taste in capitalist countries and that the media and other institutions in society play a role in both generating our alienation and shaping our taste.

Figure 4.3: Franz Kafka

Pappenheim offers an example of alienation in his discussion of the novels of Franz Kafka and also considers the impact of alienation on American culture and society. Pappenheim writes (1967:34):

> Man's alienation and his anonymous way of existing have been described with methodic and terrifying precision by Kafka, who wrote of himself: "I am separated from all things by a hollow space, and I do not even reach to its boundaries." The main characters in the novels *The Trial* and *The Castle* are completely depersonalized and reduced to mere masks. This loss of identity leads to a state of radical anonymity, which the author symbolizes by not using a name but merely a letter of the alphabet to refer to them. American novelists also have described man's fate of alienation and homelessness. We shall mention only Thomas Wolfe, who devotes much of his work to recording the painful experiences of the uprooted man, the nostalgic exile and wanderer…. Many individuals have found their own lives portrayed in Arthur Miller's Death of a Salesman. It shows Willy Loman, the "other-directed man" personified—striving all his life to be popular and "liked" but remaining absolutely lonesome and irrelevant, forever dreaming that "personality always wins the day" but in reality, destined, as his wife fears, "to fall into his grave like an old dog."

Pappenheim suggests that while alienation existed in previous ages (1967:16), "it has gained in intensity and significance in the modern world." He also offers chapters on technology and alienation, politics and alienation, social structure on alienation, and on whether alienation can be overcome.

We can overcome alienation, he suggests, but to do so, we need to change our societies, which are now dominated by the Capitalist commodity structure. It is our alienation from ourselves and others, Marxists argue, that has led to our consumer cultures and we attempt to deal with our alienation by participating in this consumer culture. Max Weber, the great German sociologist, hinted at the alienation people in America feel and felt that Americans had gone overboard in their materialistic pursuit of wealth and status symbols.

Haug on Commodity Aesthetics

Wolfgang Fritz Haug, another German Marxist, suggests that those who control the industries in capitalist societies have learned to fuse sexuality onto commodities. This has enabled them to gain greater control of that aspect of people's lives that is of most interest to the ruling classes—the purchasing of goods and services.

Haug writes in his book, *Commodity Aesthetics, Ideology and Culture*, that the advertising industry, which functions as the servant of capitalist interests, has learned how to alter human need and instinct structures—and, in doing so, I would add, affect if not shape human taste.

He writes, in his PostScript to the eighth German edition of the book, (1986:11):

> It would be particularly absurd in the case of commodity aesthetics to ignore the fact that its current dominant form is the aesthetics of the monopoly-commodity, i.e., the form in which transnational enterprises in particular intervene directly in the collective imagination of cultures.

Haug points out how the ruling classes, the bourgeoisie, benefit from protesters, since capital needs innovation. In a different book, *Critique of Commodity Aesthetics: Appearance, Sexuality, and Advertising in Capitalist Society*, he explains (1986:90):

> Young buyers are particularly ideal because they respond quickly to what is new, and are malleable and suggestible in both an active and a passive sense. Second, at the same time, it is they who constantly develop new forms and styles and offer a base of subculture from which capital can draw inspiration for fashion renewal. Most of all, some opposition groups among the young are highly productive for capital in an informal way. They consider their lifestyle to be set apart from the establishment; in so far as they make questions of appearance in lifestyle a point of criticism, they continually develop new appearances which are for a time their own—intended to identify them as a group— but which are constantly expropriated. Each new trend of aesthetic self-expression among the young automatically opens up a new market which, from the standpoint of the capitalist market, functions as a testing ground,

Eventually, Haug adds, capital takes these new styles and uses them to sell goods with the appropriated styles in the general market. So the ruling classes even benefit from those protesting the status quo and the control of society by the bourgeoisie.

Haug argues that this power to use the appearance of products (the aestheticization of commodities) and to adapt styles from youthful protest groups is now a worldwide phenomenon, and people in many countries are affected by it as it intervenes in their cultures by capturing, so to speak, people's imaginations and shaping what we might call their taste structures.

People have the illusion that they make their own decisions about what to purchase, that is, their taste, but, if Haug is right, these decisions are made for them by the way objects are sexualized and made appealing to a remarkable degree.

Figure 4.4: Jean-François Lyotard

LYoTARo

The Postmodern Problematic

It is generally held that there was a major shift or mutation in society in the mid-sixties and our modernist societies were replaced by postmodern societies. Postmodernism involves a kind of cultural de-differentiation. It developed at the same time that consumer capitalism became a cultural dominant, which explains why postmodernism is associated with consumer culture and mass consumption, which affects fashion and influences and shapes everyone's lifestyles. Postmodernism is intimately connected to the system it rejected and replaced—modernism.

One of the most famous descriptions of postmodernism is found in Jean-François Lyotard's *The Postmodern Condition: A Report on Knowledge.* University of Minnesota Press. (1984:xxiv):

> Simplifying to the extreme, I define *postmodern* as incredulity toward metanarratives. This incredulity is undoubtedly a product of progress in the sciences: but that progress in turn presupposes it. To the obsolescence

of the metanarrative apparatus of legitimation corresponds, most notably, the crisis of metaphysical philosophy and of the university institution, which in the past relied on it. The narrative function is losing its functors, its great hero, its great dangers, its great voyages, its great goal.

Lyotard calls attention to the rejection of metanarratives, the systems of philosophy and thought that dominated life in modernism—a belief in progress, philosophy, rationality, logic, and institutions. And, I should add, standards of taste.

Steven Best and Douglas Kellner offer additional insights in their book, *Postmodern Theory: Critical Interrogations* (1991:19):

Postmodern discourses thus denote new artistic, cultural, or theoretical perspectives which renounce modern discourses and practices. All of these "post" terms function as sequential markers, designating that which follows and comes after the modern. The discourse of postmodernism thus involves periodizing terms which describe a set of key changes in history, society, culture, and thought. The confusion involved in the discourse of the postmodern results from its usage in different fields and disciplines and the fact that most theorists and commentators on postmodern discourse provide definitions and conceptualizations that are frequently at odds with each other and usually inadequately theorized. Moreover, some theorists and commentators use the term postmodernism descriptively, to describe new phenomena, while others use it prescriptively, urging the adoption of new theoretical, cultural, and political discourses and practices.

An American sociologist, Todd Gitlin, provides a list of important postmodernist architects, artists, musicians, and writers in his article "Postmodernism Defined, At Last," published in *The New York Times* (Nov. 6, 1988):

A Postmodern Trope

One postmodernist trope is the list, as if culture were a garage sale, so it is appropriate to evoke postmodernism by offering a list of examples, for better or worse: Michael Graves's Portland Building, Philip Johnson's AT&T, and hundreds of more or less skillful derivatives; Robert Rauschenberg's silkscreens, Warhol's multiple-image paintings, photo-realism, Larry Rivers' erasures and pseudo-pageantry, Sherrie Levine's photographs of "classic" photographs; Disneyland, Las Vegas, suburban strips, shopping malls, mirror-glass building facades, William Burroughs, Tom Wolfe, Donald Barthelme, Monty Python, Don DeLillo, Joe Isuzu "He's lying commercials," Philip Glass, *Star Wars*, Spalding Gray, David Hockney ("Surface is illusion, but so is depth"), Max Headroom, Twyla

Tharp (choreographic Beach Boys and Frank Sinatra songs), Italo Calvino, *The Gospel of Colonus,* Robert Wilson, the Flying Karamazov Brothers, George Coates, the Kronos Quartet, Frederic Barthelme, MTV, *Miami Vice.....*

Gitlin's list is full of discussions of the way postmodernism affects our aesthetics and culture, and by implication our taste, in many areas such as literature, television programs, and architecture. We can see that people in a postmodern world think and behave differently than they did in the modernist world that preceded it. Some culture theorists argue, now, that we live in a post-postmodern world, but nobody has figured out what to call it.

Lyotard offers us an example of the importance of taste to postmodernists with his discussion of eclecticism and the postmodernist lifestyle (1984:76):

Eclecticism is the degree zero of contemporary general culture: one listens to reggae, watches a western, eats McDonald's food for lunch and local cuisine for dinner, wears Paris perfume in Tokyo, and "retro" clothes in Hong Kong; knowledge is a matter for TV games. It is easy to find a public for eclectic works. By becoming kitsch, art panders to the confusion which reigns in the "taste" of patrons. Artists, gallery owners, critics, and the public wallow together in the "anything goes," and the epoch is one of slackening.

Notice the many elements of taste in this passage. Postmodernism is brand conscious (McDonald's), style conscious ("retro clothes" in Hong Kong) and place conscious, "Paris perfume in Tokyo."

Figure 4.5: McDonald's™

Photo by the author.

Some scholars with Marxist tendencies see postmodernism as just another advanced form of capitalism, what we might call capitalism in the sheep's clothing of postmodernism. However you wish to think about it, there is no question about the impact postmodern thought has had on our lifestyles and thus on our taste, which is how we manifest our socio-economic status, among other things.

Part II:
Taste in Everyday Life

A Note on Methodology

This part of the book deals with the way taste informs our choices in many aspects of everyday life, such as the kinds of dogs we like, the cruises we take, the kinds and brands of yogurt we prefer, singers we love or hate, and so on. What we find is that we are generally overwhelmed with what we might call the "tyranny of choice," with different models and brands of devices, different brands and kinds of yogurt, different pop singers, and so on. Taste always manifests itself in things we do and products we purchase, which is why the topic is of such interest to marketers and scholars involved in studying consumer cultures.

My analyses are informed by the use of the disciplines discussed in the first part of the book: semiotics, psychoanalytic theory, sociological theory, and Marxist theory. In addition, you will find many quotations from writers and thinkers who have interesting things to say about whatever topic is being analyzed. Each discussion begins with quotations relevant to the subject being analyzed. We start with a discussion of some "micro-manifestations" of choice and taste that we all experience every day, such as which end do we crack open when eating a soft-boiled egg?

Which two mighty powers have, as I was going to tell you, been engaged in a most obstinate war for six-and-thirty moons past. It began upon the following occasion. It is allowed on all hands, that the primitive way of breaking eggs, before we eat them, was upon the larger end; but his present majesty's grandfather, while he was a boy, going to eat an egg, and breaking it according to the ancient practice, happened to cut one of his fingers. Whereupon the emperor his father published an edict, commanding all his subjects, upon great penalties, to break the smaller end of their eggs. The people so highly resented this law, that our histories tell us, there have been six rebellions raised on that account; wherein one emperor lost his life, and another his crown. These civil commotions were constantly fomented by the monarchs of Blefuscu; and when they were quelled, the exiles always fled for refuge to that empire. It is computed that eleven thousand persons have at several times suffered death, rather than submit to break their eggs at the smaller end. Many hundred large volumes have been published upon this controversy: but the books of the Big-Endians have been long forbidden, and the whole party rendered incapable by law of holding employments. During the course of these troubles, the emperors of Blefuscu did frequently expostulate by their ambassadors, accusing us of making a schism in religion, by offending against a fundamental doctrine of our great prophet Lustrog, in the fifty-fourth chapter of the Blundecral (which is their Alcoran).

Jonathan Swift. *Gulliver's Travels.*

Chapter 5

Micro Manifestations of Taste

We seldom think about it, but every morning we have many choices to make—choices reflecting our preferences and tastes, operating but hidden in the background. These choices are micro-manifestations of taste.

Figure 5.1: Traditional American Breakfast

01/04/2015

Photo by the author.

A traditional American breakfast used to include orange juice (or some other kind of juice), bacon, eggs, coffee or tea, and toast or English muffin. This photo is of a part of my breakfast served on a Princess cruise ship. On cruises, it was often possible also to have yogurt and strawberries, croissant and sweet rolls, and papaya.

What to Eat for Breakfast

For example, people who eat eggs at breakfast have to decide whether they want them fried, scrambled, poached, or boiled. Those who like soft-boiled eggs, have to decide which end to open the egg—the little end or the big end. They also have to decide how long to boil the egg to make a soft-boiled egg. My preference is for soft-boiled eggs cooked for five minutes and forty-five seconds but some people, who like runny egg whites, cook them for shorter periods of time.

Figure 5.2: Little-Endian and Big-Endian Soft-Boiled Eggs

Photo by the author.

Swift's brilliant satire on the matter of which end of the egg to use is a real masterpiece that shows how trivial things can lead to catastrophic events and is an insightful study of the human condition.

But the decision about our eggs (if we decided to have eggs for breakfast) comes only after we've made many other choices, from the moment we wake up. Do we put our stockings on, starting with our left foot or our right foot? Then, for those who wear pants, do we put our left leg or our right leg into our pants first?

We have to decide whether to go to breakfast in our pajamas and a bathrobe or get dressed, so we are ready to face the day immediately after breakfast.

When we brush our teeth, we have to decide if we should use an electronic toothbrush or a plain toothbrush, which brand of toothpaste to use, where to start brushing our teeth—in the lower-left side of our mouth, the upper-left side of our mouth, the lower-right side of our mouth or the upper right side of our mouth. And do we brush clockwise or counter-clockwise?

Many people have coffee or tea with their breakfast. We have to decide whether we like coffee or tea and regardless of which we choose, whether we want our coffee or tea with milk or not, and with or without sugar. Some people have hot cocoa and many teenagers, so I understand, have a can of soda pop.

There is also the matter of what we eat with our coffee or tea (or cocoa or whatever else we drink). Many people have a slice of toast with their morning beverage or a variant of toast, a bagel. If people prefer bagels, there are many different kinds of bagels: plain, onion, blueberry, cinnamon, and so on. Some prefer sweet rolls or muffins, of which there are countless varieties.

We don't think about these things because we develop routines that enable us to avoid having to make micro-decisions about all the things we do all the time.

But these taste routines all are based on choices we made and decided to follow and many of these choices I suggest are based on taste preferences that become habits.

Figure 5.3: Oatmeal with Chia Seeds and Ground Flax Seeds and Hot Milk

Photo by the author.

Many people have cereal in the morning and so they have to decide whether they prefer hot cereal or cold cereal. If they choose cold cereal, there are countless different kinds and brands for them to choose from. I like hot cereal and have been eating oatmeal most mornings for sixty years. There are different kinds of oatmeal to choose from. I happen to prefer traditional rather than quick-cooking oatmeal. Fruit-flavored oatmeal with sugar may be delicious, but it isn't as good for you as you think it is. I add chia seeds and ground flax seeds to my oatmeal because of their health benefits. I also have half a bagel toasted and often have a soft-boiled egg cooked for five minutes and 45 seconds. All these decisions are examples of taste preference people have. There has been, as you might imagine, an enormous amount of research on food preferences of people. We must also remember that every taste preference involves the rejection of other possible preferences, so what we don't like is also of great interest to everyone involved in consumer cultures.

Chapter 6

Yogurt

A Lesson in Home Economics: Yogurt

Figure 6.1: Instant Pot

Photo by the author.

Now for a lesson in home economics. Many Instant Pots, electronic pressure cookers, have a button that you can use to make yogurt. But you cannot use that button with regular milk—only with special kinds of milk, such as the milk sold at Dollar Tree stores that has been heated to a high temperature. Any brand of milk that doesn't need to be refrigerated probably will work. If you wish to use regular milk, you have to heat it in the Instant Pot and then let it cool down to a certain temperature before you add the yogurt and then let it sit for eight hours.

If you use milk that does not have to be refrigerated, you can put the milk in an Instant Pot with a yogurt button, add a tablespoon of yogurt, and press the yogurt button and eight hours later you will have excellent yogurt. The milk used to cost me $1.00 a quart but the Dollar Store raised the price to $1.25 a quart.

This means it costs me $.2.50 and a few cents for the yogurt, to make half a gallon of yogurt. Supermarket yogurt ordinarily costs between fifty and seventy-five cents for six ounces, and more for certain brands of yogurt.

Figure 6.2: Two Quart Jar of Yogurt made with Instant Pot

Photo by the author.

We can contrast my yogurt with Straus yogurt, a very upscale brand of yogurt, that costs a great deal more than my homemade yogurt.

Figure 6.3: Straus™ Organic Yogurt

Photo by the author.

This brand of yogurt, from Straus dairies, costs $5.99 for 32 ounces at supermarkets and is relatively expensive. At one of my supermarkets, you can buy two quarts of yogurt for $5.00. So, I am saving around $3.00 every time I make yogurt. My Instant Pot cost $60, which means after I make yogurt twenty times, the Instant Pot has paid for itself. I learned about using Dollar Tree milk from a video on YouTube, which has dozens of videos on making yogurt with an Instant Pot.

Yogurt in its natural state, without fruit and sugar, is a legitimate health food. But most people buy flavored yogurt because they prefer its taste. Flavored yogurt usually has three or four teaspoons of sugar and some fruit in a small container. They are getting some health benefits from eating yogurt but also consuming a considerable amount of sugar.

Chapter 7

Dogs

The *World Canine Organization* is best known by its French title Fédération Cynologique Internationale (FCI). It is the largest registry of dog breeds that is internationally accepted. At the time of this writing, the FCI recognizes 339 breeds of dogs, which are divided into 10 groups based on the dog's purpose or function or on its appearance or size. The 10 groups are:

1. Sheepdogs and Cattle Dogs, other than Swiss Cattle Dogs (this group includes most of the dogs found classified as "herding dogs" by other kennel clubs).

2. Pinscher and Schnauzer, Molossoid Breeds, Swiss Mountain and Cattle Dogs and Other Breeds (the Molossian breeds include the dogs known as the mastiffs by most other kennel clubs)

3. Terriers

4. Dachshunds

5. Spitz and Primitive Types

6. Scenthounds and Related Breeds

7. Pointers and Setters

8. Retrievers, Flushing Dogs, Water Dogs

9. Companion and Toy Dogs

10. Sighthounds

Each group is divided into subgroups of dog breeds and each has been assigned a country or region of origin. While the country listed may not be the very first place where the dog breed appeared, it is usually the first nation to have recognized and registered the breed and currently is the home of the breed organization that determines the standard of these breeds, which is the description of the ideal qualities of a dog of that particular breed. You will probably find some surprises in this list, such as that the Australian Shepherd is actually a breed created in the United States, while the Pharaoh Hound was not developed in Egypt, but in Malta.

If you decide to get a dog, you really will be confronted by the tyranny of choice. There are, as we read above, 339 different breeds of dogs, plus countless varieties of mutts that are mixes of breeds. We have many choices, perhaps an overwhelming number of choices, to make when getting a dog, if choosing the "right" breed of dog is an important matter for us. If you decide to get a mixed-breed dog from the pound, life is a lot simpler, and the dog is a lot less expensive.

The Evolution of Dogs

Here is an article about the evolution of dogs from the Morris Animal Foundation website:

> Thanks to thousands of years of human interaction and intervention, today we have a large variety of dog breeds proudly strutting across our television screens and our living rooms. The story of how dogs have evolved from wolf to Chihuahua is a fascinating one that starts with our respective ancestors' earliest encounters/
>
> Most researchers who study canine genetics agree that dogs are really domesticated wolves – after all, their scientific name is *Canis lupus familiaris*. But the exact time that the relationship between wolves and humans turned from distrust and fear to a mutually beneficial partnership is disputed. A large body of research suggests that dogs were domesticated between 12,500 and 15,000 years ago, but recent genetic studies suggest that domestication might have taken place even earlier. Some researchers believe dogs might have comingled with humans as early as 130,000 years ago, long before our human ancestors settled into agricultural communities.
>
> https://www.morrisanimalfoundation.org/article/evolution-of-dogs

During the pandemic, many people who ordinarily would not be interested in having a dog got them to provide company for themselves and their families. Why people get dogs and why they get the dogs they get is an interesting problem for anyone interested in taste. Sometimes, people go to a pound and choose any dog that they think is cute or manifests personality characteristics they like. But other people spend a good deal of time deciding what kind of dog to get and, in some cases, spend a lot of money to purchase pure-breed dogs. In these cases, taste plays an important role.

My wife and I got a dog, "Patches," a female Cockapoo, many years ago because, like many people, we thought it would be good for our children to have a dog. We had her for seventeen years and when she died, we concluded that we didn't want the responsibility of having a pet any longer. I understand many people feel the same way.

Some Hypotheses About People's Taste in Dogs

I offer here some hypotheses about people's taste in dogs, whether purebred or not, and how dogs function in families (assuming the dog is not neurotic and the owner or family that has the dog is normal. In many cases, sad to say, the dog is normal, but the family is not).

Hypothesis 1.
Dogs are substitute children.

Many people treat their dogs like children and for them the dog functions as that most wonderful of things, the "child" who obeys. That is, if the dog has been trained correctly. Dogs are seen as members of the family. The Pope recently complained that too many Catholics were getting dogs and not having children. One reason for that is that it costs around $275,000 or more to raise a child in a middle-class family to age 18, and a dog is a lot cheaper.

Hypothesis 2.
Dogs elevate the sense of power of their owners.

For many people, dogs, if trained properly, generally obey commands. This has a psychological benefit for people who have unconscious needs for a sense of power over someone or something. Dogs then help people deal with their unconscious command imperatives or command needs. Some breeds of dogs, such as pit bulls, reflect an unconscious sense of power in their owners from their ability to intimidate other breeds of dogs and, in some cases, other people.

Hypothesis 3.
Dogs provide unconditional love.

Dogs provide constant affection and love to those with whom they live, regardless of how they are treated. In addition, this love is unconditional—not based on love as a reward for achievement, the way many of the masters of the dogs were raised.

Hypothesis 4.
Dogs have personalities.

Unlike cats, which show (at least overtly) relatively little personality, dogs of all kinds have well-developed personalities and often provide amusement and entertainment for their owners. TikTok is full of videos showing how different facets of personality are found in dogs and how amusing dogs can be.

Hypothesis 5:

Dogs help their owners satisfy their need for attention.

Some dogs, such as very small dogs, unusual breeds of dogs, and enormous dogs such as Great Danes, attract attention and thus provide gratification to their owners as far as narcissistic needs for being noticed are concerned. People walking dogs often talk with people they meet, which means that dogs provide an important means of socializing.

Dogs and Health

What follows is not a hypothesis, but a matter of scientific fact. Harvard University's health site on the Internet has an article titled,

> "Get Healthy, Get a Dog: The health benefits of canine companionship," that offers the following information about the health benefits of having dogs:
>
> This Special Health Report, *Get Healthy, Get a Dog: The health benefits of canine companionship* shows how having a dog can also reduce feelings of isolation and loneliness, help calm jagged nerves, and improve the lives of older individuals. Just petting a dog can lower the petter's blood pressure and heart rate (while having a positive effect on the dog as well).
>
> There are many reasons why dogs are called humans' best friends: not only do they offer unparalleled companionship, but a growing body of research shows they also boost human health. Owning a dog can prompt you to be more physically active — have leash, will walk. It can also:
>
> - help you be calmer, more mindful, and more present in your life
> - make kids more active, secure, and responsible
> - improve the lives of older individuals
> - make you more social and less isolated
>
> *Get Healthy, Get a Dog,* a Special Health Report from Harvard Medical School, details the many ways that dogs can improve the lives of humans.
>
> https://www.health.harvard.edu/staying-healthy/get-healthy-get-a-dog

We see, then, that having a dog has many health benefits for individuals and their families, which may explain why so many people have dogs for pets, despite the cost.

Statistics of Dog and Cat Ownership

Here are statistics about dog and cat ownership in the United States.

	Dogs	**Cats**
Percent of households owning	38.4	25.4
Number of households owning	48 million	31 million
Average number owned per household	1.6	1.8
Total number in United States	76 million	58 million
Veterinary visits per household per year (mean)	2.4	1.3
Veterinary expenditure per household per year (mean)	$410	$182
Veterinary expenditure per animal (mean)	$253	$98

https://www.avma.org/resources-tools/reports-statistics/us-pet-ownership-statistics.

This material was accessed on 12/30/2021. I don't know how accurate or up-to-date it is, but it provides a good overview of pet ownership in the United States and what it costs to own a dog or a cat.

The Cost of Having a Dog

An article on the Internet on "Pet Budget" offers the following information:

Most puppies cost between $500 and $2,500 ($1,300 on average). But it is possible to adopt a dog for $50 to $500. On average, dog owners will spend around $140/month ($33/week) on essential expenses for their pet, which will add up to $21,000 throughout the dog's lifetime.

Additionally, costs like insurance ($565 per year on average), spaying or neutering ($100 to $500), dog walking ($15 to $50 per walk), or boarding services ($25 to $85 per day) would increase the cost of ownership as well. It is also essential to know that prices can vary significantly depending on products and services quality and your location.

https://www.petbudget.com/dog-cost/

My daughter's dog, a sweet but not too intelligent Great Dane, ate a sock one day and needed a $6000 operation. So emergencies can be quite expensive. If I recall correctly, they had dog insurance, so they escaped from a huge bill. Cats are much less expensive. According to the ASPCA, cats cost around $640 a year.

The moral of this disquisition is that love, wherever you find it, always costs a good deal more than you think it will. But it is worth it.

Figure 7.1: Whitney

Photo by the author.

Whitney. A Case Study:

Whitney is a dog owned by our neighbors. Here are the answers they gave to some questions I asked them:

1. What breed is it?

Labrador retriever with a touch of Pit Bull

2. Why did you decide to get that breed of dog?

Our first rescue dog (an Australian cattle dog) became difficult to manage, so we reluctantly surrendered him back to the SF SPCA. After a grieving period, we went back to various Bay Area rescues looking for a breed that might have a better temperament. We found Whitney, who looked like a Labrador retriever, and adopted her.

3. What is its name? Why did you choose that name?

Whitney, after Mount Whitney

4. How has it affected your life? What benefits are you getting from having it? Has it caused any problems?

We love how a dog keeps us more active through walks, running, and hiking; exploring new outdoor spaces we wouldn't normally go to (e.g. Fort Funston!), and seeing her interact with us and our firstborn. Problems include financial as pets can be expensive when it comes to their medical and boarding costs. Whitney doesn't get along with every dog, so we have to manage her with treats when we are on walks or hikes. Whitney is also an anxious dog, so we avoid crowded spaces where she is unable to relax.

On Google, there was an article saying that the cost of purchasing a purebred Labrador Retriever averages around $800 (the range is $400 to $1500), so dogs can be expensive to buy and they cost a considerable amount of money to keep. Having a dog offers many pleasures but it also can offer many challenges. For most people who get dogs, the pleasures obviously outweigh the challenges and the cost.

Chapter 8

Celine Dion

Who Is Celine Dion?

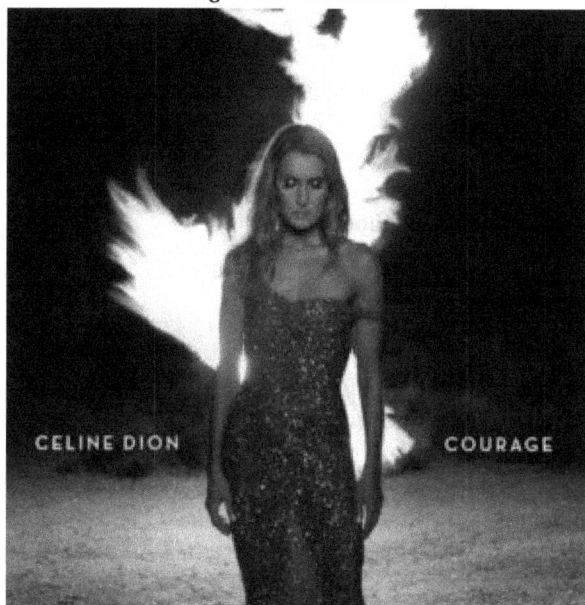

Photo from her website, https://www.celinedion.com/.

A star from a young age, singer Celine Dion had recorded nine French albums and won numerous awards by the time she was 18. She delivered her first English-language album, *Unison*, in 1990. Dion's real breakthrough into pop music stardom came in 1992 when she recorded the theme to Disney's hit animated feature *Beauty and the Beast*. She went on to record several hits, including four No. 1's: "The Power of Love," "Because You Loved Me," "My Heart Will Go On" and "I'm Your Angel."

By 18, Dion had recorded nine French albums and won numerous Felix and Juno awards, the Canadian equivalent of a Grammy Award. In 1988, she won the Eurovision Song Contest in Dublin, Ireland, and her performance was broadcast live in countries throughout Europe, the Middle East, Australia, and Japan. After this taste of international acclaim, she began looking to the south and American stardom. Dion recorded her first English-language album, *Unison*, in 1990. Like most of her English-language albums, it was a collaboration with the songwriter-arranger-musician David Foster. Driven by the Top 5 single "Where Does My Heart Beat Now," *Unison* sold more than one million copies. Dion's real breakthrough into pop music stardom came in 1992, when she recorded the theme to Disney's hit animated feature *Beauty and the Beast*, a duet with Peabo Bryson. The song, "Beauty and the Beast," made it to No. 9 on the Billboard Hot 100 and won both a Grammy and an Academy Award.

https://www.biography.com/musician/celine-dion

Celine Dion is the subject of a book by Carl Wilson about taste that deals with her album,"Let's Talk About Love". The title of Wilson's book is *Let's Talk About Love: A Journey to the End of Taste.*

Carl Wilson's Book: Let's Talk About Love

Here is a discussion of Wilson's book in a February 15, 2008 article by Jim Emerson, "A Journey to the End of Taste."

> Wilson's real obsession here is not Céline but the thorny philosophical problem on which her reputation has been impaled: the nature of taste itself. What motivates aesthetic judgment? Is our love or hatred of "My Heart Will Go On" the result of a universal, disinterested instinct for beauty-assessment, as Kant would argue? Or is it something less exalted? Wilson tends to side with the French sociologist Pierre Bourdieu, who argues that taste is never disinterested: It's a form of social currency, or "cultural capital," that we use to stockpile prestige. Hating Céline is therefore not just an aesthetic choice, but an ethical one, a way to elevate yourself above her fans—who, according to market research, tend to be disproportionately poor adult women living in flyover states and shopping at big-box stores. (As Wilson puts it, "It's hard to imagine an audience that could confer less cool on a musician.")

Another article about the book is from Edward Keenan in Toronto's *Eye Weekly* ("Let's talk about contempt"):

> … [W]hen Wilson talks about Let's Talk About Love, he's really talking about the way we relate to each other as human beings. Readers of the dizzyingly dweeby intellectualizing that often makes Wilson's blog an exhausting pleasure to read will not be surprised that, for him, a discussion of the love theme from Titanic must encompass an examination of Quebecois culture, the history of parlour entertainment as it relates to the immigrant experience, the philosophies of Hume and Kant.

Wilson's reading of philosophy, social theory and his own conscience pretty conclusively demonstrates that the revulsion Dion inspires in the cultural elite is a function of class. We like what we like because of our social circle and education and cultural and economic prospects, and we dislike most intensely that which we perceive to be beneath our station.

In other words, Keenan points out, what we call "taste" has a lot to do with shame, and is intertwined with issues of age, class, and race, that we label conveniently as separate concerns. How we feel about Celine Dion and her songs, and singers like her, and by extension, much of popular culture is tied to our revulsion about the taste of social classes that we feel are beneath us.

Wilson's book, whose subtitle "A Journey to the End of Taste," deals with Dion's reputation and other aspects of her career. He quotes a British sociologist Simon Frith, who wrote that Dion is (2007:14):

> Probably the most loathed superstar I can remember, at least by everyone I know, not just critics but even my mother-in-law...I doubt if she will ever be redeemed ABBA-style, and what seems to concern everyone is that she is just naft.

Dion, Wilson points out, has sold 175 million albums and is the twenty-third best-selling singer of all time. She is also the most successful singer in the French language and may even be the best-selling female singer. She has a nightly review in Las Vegas that has been sold out for four years.

Why Some Critics Dislike Celine Dion

Clearly, Dion is enormously popular, and she's popular all over the world, but for music critics like Wilson, she is popular with the wrong kind of people because of the nature of her singing (described on the back cover of the book as "tear-jerking sentimentality") and the kind of songs she sings. Wilson explains his feelings about her (2007:17):

> My aversion to Dion more closely resembles how put off I feel when someone says they're pro-life or a Republican: intellectually I'm aware how personal and complicated such affiliations are more crudely tribal.

> Musical subcultures exist because our guts tell us certain kinds of music are for certain kinds of people. The codes are not always transparent. We are attracted to a song's beat, its edge, its warmth, its idiosyncrasy, the singer's *je ne sais quoi; We* check out the music our friends or cultural guides commend.

Wilson describes Dion's singing as being like schmaltz (rendered chicken fat), as having no personality, and as being bland. He writes (2007:69):

> Her singing itself is aspirational, reaching out palpably in vocal curlicues and unfurling bolts, like overstuffed furniture festooned with a fat flower pattern. Her voice itself is *nouveau right*. It's a volume business. No wonder middle-class critics find it gauche.

Carl Wilson on Pierre Bourdieu

Figure 8.2: Pierre Bourdieu

His chapter "Let's Talk About Whose Got Bad Taste," deals with sociologist Pierre Bourdieu (2007:88-89):

> Bourdieu's interpretation was that tastes were serving as strategic tools. While working-class tastes seemed mainly a default (serving at best to express group belongingness and solidarity), for everyone else taste was not only a product of economic and educational background but as it developed through life, a force mobilized as part of their quest for social status (or what Bourdieu called symbolic power). What we have agreed to call tastes, he said, is an array of symbolic associations we use to set ourselves apart from those whose social ranking is beneath us, and to take aim at the status we think we deserve. Taste is a means of distinguishing ourselves from others, the pursuit of *distinction*.

It is what Bourdieu describes as our cultural capital that determines whether we love or hate Celine Dion. Later in the chapter, Wilson discusses Dion's audience, who tend to be over fifty and almost seventy percent female—a very uncool audience. It is because Dion is so uncool that Wilson dislikes her singing. Dion herself, Wilson writes, seems to be a very nice person. It is only when she opens her mouth to sing that problems arise for Wilson but not for her millions of adoring fans, who, it is suggested, shop at big box stores and live lives of quiet desperation in flyover parts of America.

The Culture Wars: Why is Popular Culture So Unpopular?

The answer to this question is that popular culture is popular with large numbers of people, but is not popular with some elites who wish to distance themselves from socio-economic classes they feel are "beneath" them. As Bourdieu explains in *Sociology in Question* (1993:105):

> I will not surprise anyone by saying that a person's social class, of "class" (as in he's got class) can be identified infallibly from his preferred music (or simply the radio station he listens to) as from the apéritif—Pernod, Martini or whisky—that he drinks.

So our taste in music is an important signifier of one's socio-economic class. The epigraph to this book quotes Bourdieu to the effect that taste, personal opinion, and the idea of personal taste are an illusion. Taste, we may say, is socially constructed and is connected to chance matters such as the family one is born in, subcultures to which people belong, and similar phenomena.

Popular culture is a term used to identify certain kinds of texts, generally mass-mediated, that appeal to many people. Some mass communication theorists often identify "popular" with "mass" and suggest that if something is popular, it must be of poor quality, appealing to the mythical "lowest common denominator." Or, another way to put it, "low-brow" culture. Popular culture is generally held to be the opposite of elite culture—arts that require certain levels of sophistication and refinement to be appreciated, such as ballet, opera, poetry, and classical music. In this postmodern age, many critics now question this popular culture/elite culture polarity.

Typologies of Taste

Sociologists and culture critics of all kinds have made many differed typologies involving people's taste. An article by Thomas Mallon in the Jul 29, 2014 issue of *The New York Times*, "Highbrow, Lowbrow, Middlebrow — Do These Kinds of Cultural Categories Mean Anything Anymore?" offers us an overview of this topic:

> According to the world's No. 1 unibrow reference tool, Wikipedia, the term "highbrow" was popularized in 1902 by Will Irvin, a reporter for the New York newspaper. The Sun, who "adhered to the phrenological notion of more intelligent people having high foreheads." A certain whiff of racialism and eugenics should have been enough to do in this word by now, but it has retained a smidgen of utility in a culture that still likes to rank the prestige of artistic endeavors.
>
> "Highbrow" spawned "lowbrow" and "middlebrow," the last of these standing for something blandly conventional, lacking either refined distinction or raw energy. Dwight Macdonald, giving the terms a postwar freshening and some sociological heft, defined the massive terrain of "Midcult" in 1960 as a "middlebrow compromise" that "pretends to respect the standards of High Culture while in fact it waters them down and vulgarizes them."

There is one more concept relative to brows and culture made by an anonymous writer, "What is Nobrow? Is it Different From Postbrow?" which argues on a site "Thought Catalogue":

> Thought Catalog is, per its self-description, "nobrow." But what is nobrow? According to The Art and Popular Culture Encyclopedia (whose Wikipedia-style entry on nobrow I found via Google, and which, I presume, is a very legitimate source), nobrow is "a postmodern neologism derived from highbrow and lowbrow" and was coined by John Seabrook in his book *Nobrow: The Culture of Marketing, the Marketing of Culture* (2000).
>
> In the context of intellectual discourse, nobrow indicates influence from both high and low culture. A nobrow person thinks that "good," "valuable" art or thought can derive from high- or middle- or lowbrow culture (or a mixture of these). Nobrow is a more inclusive taste in culture. But while it validates art that might previously have been ignored by critics, nobrow still operates within the system of terms ("high," "low") that created such disparity. Even if you're rebelling against your parents' ideas, it's hard to leave them completely behind.
>
> https://thoughtcatalog.com/anonymous/2010/10/what-is-nobrow-is-it-different-than-postbrow

With "nobrow" we reach a fitting conclusion to the use of "brows" to categorize works of elite art and popular culture. We must recognize that these broad typologies are based on spurious notions about what art is and what is behind the various typologies: a feeling of superiority on the part of those who like highbrow culture relative to the general public.

There is another taste typology, U and Non-U, that is also quite controversial. Arguments about U and Non-U were set in motion by an article by Nancy Mitford. An article in *Tatler* by Matthew Bell, "U and Non-U: How to be upper class in 2019: Yorkshire Tea? In. Trophy spouses? Out. Don't put a foot wrong with the new-U rules," discusses this topic:

> Nancy Mitford has a lot to answer for. It was she who, in 1955, set out in print what had never been written before—the unspoken rules for being 'U' or upper-class, and 'non-U'. Her article, published in the CIA-funded magazine *Encounter*, provoked an outcry, not least from her old friend Evelyn Waugh. In an open letter denouncing her for lobbing this grenade into British society, he wrote: 'There are subjects too intimate for print. Surely class is one?'
>
> Reading Mitford's essay now, you realise how quickly everything changes. Back then, her observations on class were based on language – whether you 'took a bath' (non-U) or 'had one's bath' (U). Whether you

said 'chimneypiece' (U) or 'mantelpiece' (non-U). Today, having a bathtub at all is a sign of leisure, and therefore U (showers being much more common in every sense), while having a fireplace has become similarly recherché – and therefore U.

https://www.tatler.com/article/nancy-mitford-u-and-non-u-language

What we learn from these various taste typologies is taste has been the subject of many controversies over the years. Postmodernism, with its focus on de-differentiation, cuts the Gordian culture knot and suggests that elite culture and popular culture are not that different and thus the various cultural typologies discussed above are irrelevant.

Earlier in this chapter, one commentator explained that hating Celine Dion was a way of elevating oneself above her fans, so one's attitude towards Dion and popular culture has social dimensions of some consequence. One reason people don't like popular culture is that they don't like the kind of people who like popular culture.

We often read that "there is no disputing taste," but as this discussion of Celine Dion and the culture wars suggests, that is not always the case and many people do argue about taste for various reasons, such as class differences and a dislike of people in certain classes.

Although ships have been a means of transportation since early times, the cruise industry is young. Its purpose is really to provide a resort experience rather than point-to-point transportation. Though the modern-day cruise industry is barely 20 years old, it has established itself as an important component of the United States travel and tourism industry. A study in 1993 by the highly respected U.S. accounting firm Price Waterhouse indicated that the cruise industry has an estimated economic impact on the United States of approximately $14.5 billion annually. It is indirectly responsible for the employment of 450,000 Americans and directly responsible for the employment of 134,000....The cruise industry's performance and satisfaction are the pacesetters for the rest of the travel industry. No other vacation category can touch a cruise for product satisfaction and repeat business. (2000: 155, 156)

Charles R. Goeldner, J.R. Brent Ritchie, Robert W. McIntosh
Tourism: Principles, Practices, Philosophies (Eighth edition).
New York: Wiley. 2000.

Norwegian Prima will offer the highest staffing levels and space ratio of any new cruise ship in the contemporary and premium cruise categories, delivering an unrivaled guest experience. She will offer the largest variety of suite categories available at sea with 13 suite categories as well as the largest three-bedroom suites of any new cruise ship and the Brand's largest-ever inside, oceanview and balcony staterooms, including the Brand's largest-ever bathrooms and showers for standard stateroom categories. Norwegian Prima will also offer the most outdoor deck space of any new cruise ship including more total pool deck space than any other ship in NCL's fleet as well as multiple infinity pools and vast outdoor walkways allowing guests to take in the sea, the ocean breeze and a variety of elevated experiences.

https://www.ncl.com/newsroom/norwegian-cruise-line-unveils-much-anticipated-norwegian-prima?

Chapter 9

Ocean Cruises

The ocean cruise industry was a remarkably successful branch of the tourism industry until Covid-19 appeared on the scene in 2020 and then the industry (and all forms of tourism) experienced a traumatic two years. But in 2022, despite the problems caused by the new virus variants, the ocean cruise industry seems to be doing very well. This is the case despite warnings from the CDC. Many people are taking cruises again and disregarding the dangers posed by Covid-19.

Figure 9.1: The Norwegian Epic

Photo by the author.

Social Class and Cruising

As a rule, cruise ships don't have different classes of passengers the way ocean liners once did, but different cruise lines cater to different classes of people. The Princess Line and many other lines catering to the same kinds of passengers, such as Norwegian and Royal Caribbean, focus on middle-class cruise takers while some lines, such as Regent Seven Seas, are much more expensive and appeal to wealthy upper-class cruise takers. Now many cruise ships, such as the *Norwegian Epic*, have certain parts of the ship set aside for people who pay more than the typical passenger for special cabins and benefits. So, social class and class differentiation are returning to many mass tourism cruise liners.

A 10-day cruise on *Regent Seven Seas* on March 7, 2022, costs $17,798 according to the Regent Seven Seas brochure, and $6600 on an internet site, Vacations to Go. A 10-day ocean view cruise on Princess from San Francisco to Mexico on January 6, 2022, costs $1359 according to the brochure, and $549 on

Vacations to Go. So, the cruise on Regent Seven Seas costs about $660 a day which is more than a 10-day cruise on the Princess line.

What is remarkable about Princess Cruises and other similar premier cruise lines, is that the quality of the food is often excellent when you dine in the dining rooms, and the service is always superb. A friend of mine, who took many cruises, explained to me once, "dining on a cruise ship is like going to a decent French restaurant. And it's free."

Figure 9.2: Prime Rib Dinner Served on Star Princess on Sailaway

Photo by the author.

Categories of Cruise Ships

An important blog, AllThingCruise.com, offers the following categories of lines and ships:

Contemporary

Aida, Carnival, Costa, Celestial, Fred Olsen, P&O

Upscale Contemporary

MSC, Norwegian, Royal Caribbean, Viking

Premium

Celebrity, Disney, Holland America, Princess

Ultra Premium

Azamara, Cunard, Oceana, Windstar

Ultra Luxury

Crystal, Hapag Lloyd, Paul Gauguin, Regent Seven Seas, Seabourn, Sea Cloud, Sundream, Seven Seas, Silversea

Some analysts offer different names for the categories and may place some ships in other categories, but most typologies have the same ships as luxury or ultra-luxury cruise ships. Thus, it may be reasonable to put Viking as a premium or even an ultra-premium ship and, with the evolution of the industry, some new ships in an upscale contemporary category, such as MSC, may be best seen as a premium ship.

Nothing But the Best: Regent Seven Seas Cruises Line Brochure

The lines all publish brochures which describe what it is like to sail with them. Let me offer an example from a Regent brochure with the lines broken the same way they are in the brochure.

On the cover we read:

Regent
Seven Seas Cruises
An Unrivaled Experience

ALASKAN WILDS
& SOUTH AMERICAN
MARVELS

Alaska &
South America

Below that we read:

Return
with Regent

$1000 shipboard credit
plus
REGENT REASSURANCE

The brochure starts with four pages meant to convince potential cruise takers that sailing with Regent Seven Seas will be safe. It discusses the many safety measures Regent Seven Seas has taken to guard passengers against the coronavirus. Dealing with the anxieties that all cruise passengers feel is necessary before you can convince them of the value of sailing with them.

After this discussion of the many safeguards on their ships, there is a page titled IMMERSE YOURSELF that deals with the pleasures of ocean travel and a page with language that is worth examining in some detail. I am reproducing the text with the line breaks found in the brochure. I have highlighted, in boldface, some of the most interesting incentives for taking a cruise with Regent Seven-Seas.

> ENJOY **EVERY**
> MOMENT
> in **All-Inclusive Luxury**
>
> **Every** detail is taken care of so you **can fully** experience and
> enjoy **every** moment; this is at the heart of our **all-inclusiveness**.
>
> We **aspire** to give you more than just the **most luxurious** ships,
> **exquisite** meals, **refined** service, or **exhilarating** shore excursions.
>
> We aspire to give you more than any one of those things because
> truly all-inclusive travel is about delighting in the entire experience
> **without hassle or compromise.**
>
> Discover the **most complete**, all-inclusive experience on the
> ocean, from your suite being maintained **exactly as you'd prefer**
> to **the abundance** of **unforgettabl**e moments awaiting you with
> our FREE Unlimited Shore Excursions. And, with inclusions like
> transfers to and from your ship and business class air on
> intercontinental flights, every journey should feel planned **just**
> **for you, from beginning to end.**

This passage is full of superlatives that generate a sense of exclusiveness and luxuriousness. Consider the language used:

every moment	exhilarating shore excursions
all-inclusive	most complete
every detail	abundance
fully experience	unforgettable
aspire	awaiting
most luxurious	just for you
exquisite meals	from beginning to end
refined service	

The terms also indicate that these superlatives are unique and directed at the reader, a kind of hyper-personalization or hyper-individuation that should convince readers of the kind of specialized service they can expect on their cruise.

Passengers on Seven-Seas luxury ships don't just "experience" but "fully experience" things; their meals are "exquisite," the service is "refined," the shore excursions are "exhilarating," the all-inclusive experience is the "most complete," and a cruise on Seven-Seas ships will be "unforgettable" and all of this is "just for you." And all of this "from beginning to end." Everything is pitched in terms of totalities such as "every," "most," "unforgettable," and "from beginning to end."

For travelers looking for cruises that reflect a certain level of taste and discrimination, the Regent Seven-Seas are signifiers of sophistication and high status. These cruises are aspirational for some people looking to improve their sense of accomplishment and status, who really don't belong on these cruises in terms of their socio-economic status. They are splurging. So sailing on a super-luxury cruise is complicated, as far as status and distinction are concerned. The brochure has several other pages of text and images, such as A PERSONAL TOUCH, which deals with the service on the ship, and A TASTE FOR TRAVEL, which is devoted to the 'exquisite" food served on the ship. The remainder of the brochure lists the Alaskan and South American cruises Regent Seven Seas offers.

We can say that all levels of cruising can be considered as luxury experiences since all of one's needs are taken care of and there are excellent meals to be had, entertainment to be enjoyed, and a "carnivalesque" pleasure-seeking atmosphere on cruise ships. But there are degrees of luxury, ranging from the kind of luxury found on contemporary cruise lines (sometimes for as little as $50 a night per person) up to the kind of luxury found on ultra-luxury lines (sometimes costing $1000 or more per person).

The ocean cruise lines have been successful because they provide a remarkable experience at various price points, but even in the lowest categories of cruise lines, passengers often have satisfying and at times even extraordinary experiences.

There have been remarkable changes in the designs of cruise ships and now some cruise lines have ships that transcend the traditional categories. So, cruises on the Norwegian line's new ships are hard to classify and a cruise on the line's newest ship, like the *Prima,* is quite different from one on the line's *Epic.* The *Prima* has an enormous walking deck that represents a major departure from traditional cruise ship design.

Figure 9.3: Huge restaurant deck on Norwegian Prima

Used by permission of Norwegian Cruise Line™.

A review of the *Viva* by Adam Coulter on July 29, 2022 reads:

Take away the water slides and the three-deck racetrack and the vast casino, and you'd be hard-pressed to find anything on Norwegian Cruise Line's newest cruise ship, Norwegian Prima, that says, "mainstream cruise ship."

From the three €70,000 chandeliers in the upmarket French restaurant, Le Bistro; to the sculptures by Alexander Krivosheiw along Ocean Boulevard to the exquisite gold butterfly installations that adorn the ceiling in Hudson's, one of the ship's main dining rooms, Norwegian Prima has the look and feel of a Four Seasons or Ritz-Carlton hotel.

Which was exactly the intention, as President and CEO of Norwegian Cruise Line Holdings Frank del Rio -- who was at today's handover ceremony in Venice -- explains:

"With this ship we said: 'This is my last hurrah. I've been building ships for a long time; I've been building Oceania and Regent ships and we said we're gonna throw the kitchen sink at this vessel.'

"We're going to create a contemporary category vessel that if I blindfold you and drop you in, you'd be hard pressed to know if you were on Oceania upper premium ship or if you are on a Regent ultra-luxury ship -- and I think we've succeeded in doing that."

https://www.cruisecritic.com/news/7049/

On a cruise my wife and I took many years ago, on an old Celebrity ship, two young women in the cabin next to ours were crying as we were about to get off the ship. "We don't want to leave," one of them said. "We'd like to stay on a lot longer," the other woman added. For millions of people, ocean cruising is a pleasure and for large numbers of people, it is very much like an addiction.

Brands are taking back control. The trend we have all been suspecting is going on, through our own daily experiences, is gathering weight across adland. The latest figures from the WFA show that a majority of the world's biggest brands, some 70%, have changed media agencies in a bid to regain control of their spending. OK —so we're only talking about 35 global brands here, because the bar is set high on advertising across the planet, but between them, these brands account for a $30bn ad spend each year. So that is a lot of budget being moved to new agencies.

Sean Hargrave, *Media Post*, August 21, 2021

By the end of the 1940s, there was a burgeoning awareness that a brand wasn't just a mascot or a catchphrase or a picture printed on the label of a company's product; the company as a whole could have a brand identity or a "corporate consciousness," as this ephemeral quality was termed at the time. As this idea evolved, the adman ceased to see himself as a pitchman and instead saw himself as "the philosopher-king of commercial culture," in the words of ad critic Randall Rothberg. The search for the true meaning of brands - or the "brand essence," as it is often called - gradually took the agencies away from individual products and their attributes and toward a psychological/anthropological examination of what brands mean to the culture and to people's lives.

Naomi Klein. *No Logo.* (2002)

A Bloomberg analysis of the top 20 spots of the Billboard Hot 100 over the past three years found that the most popular brand name dropped was — somewhat unexpectedly — Rolls-Royce, which was mentioned in 11 songs. Eight of the top 12 brands are vehicles; the other four are Hennessy cognac, Nike's Air Jordan sneakers, Rolex watches, and Xanax. I really hope Xanax never makes a car.

Bloomberg. Significant Digits, August 22, 2017

Chapter 10

Brands

When it comes to ways of expressing our taste in things we buy and like, brands play an all-important role. The brands of things we own are, in semiotic terms, messages about ourselves, and everything we own or buy, with few exceptions, is branded. Not only must we consider brands, but also the various models of the brands we like.

Figure 10.1: Apple™ Logo

You do not buy an Apple watch, but a particular model of the watch, and every model choice is a sign of one's taste, sense of style, status, and identity. I wrote an article some years ago titled, "The Branded Self" which argued that our identities are based, in large measure, on the brands of things we own. Here is a brief excerpt from that paper:

The Branded Self

This paper suggests that a self, at least a public identity, can be seen, semiotically speaking, as a kind of text that is constructed, in an intertextual way, out of other people's texts, or for the purposes of this investigation, their branded fashion creations and other similarly branded commodities.

Brands, for semioticians, are what Saussure called signifiers (yet they often are identified by icons) that companies use to help establish their identities. The essence of a brand is being "different" from other brands and from generic products. Brands use advertising to establish an image of what they are and what kind of people use their products. Brands, we may say, are pure connotation. Saussure said (1915/1965:120) "in language, there are only differences." From a Saussurean perspective we can say "in brands, there are only differences." Brands compete with one another and with generic products or commodities.

I realize now that talking about brands is not enough. We must also become more granular and consider the models of objects we own or the styles of clothes we wear. Thus, we don't just own blue jeans or a brand of blue jeans but also a particular style of the brand of blue jeans we buy, or the model of a smartwatch or smartphone we buy.

Blue jeans come in styles such as straight leg, skinny, distressed, and flared. Suppose a person decides to purchase Levi's blue jeans. For men, there are models such as 550 Relaxed Fit, 501 Original Fit Jeans, 505 Regular Fit Jeans, and many other styles. If you look at the Levi's jeans available on Amazon.com you find many brands and styles of jeans from which to choose. And choice, let us remember, is central to taste.

I have an old pair of Levi's 501 jeans, whose patch I've drawn below. But, like many people, I have other brands of jeans as well. On the Internet, there is a site that reports that women, on average, own seven pairs of jeans and men own six pairs of jeans.

Figure 10.2: Patch from 501 Jeans

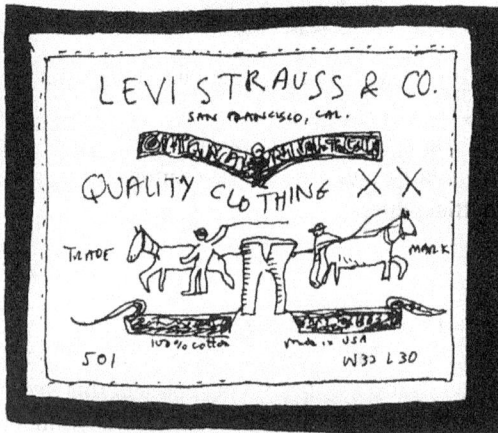

Drawing by the author.

This matter of deciding not only the brand of products we purchase but also the style and model number of that brand is a reflection of the almost infinite number of choices we have to make in purchasing clothes, smartphones, automobiles, and all the other products we use to generate a "look" creating what we might call a visual identity.

"Looks" and Poseurs

Our "looks" are all combinations of brands that convey messages to others about what we are like, our status, and other things about us. People who observe us when we are in public base their analyses on advertisements for the products we are wearing and their status, among other things. There is always the problem of poseurs--people who wear clothes above their socio-economic status or wealthy people who disguise their status by dressing like poor people. We must recall semiotician Umberto Eco's point that people can lie with signs.

A sociologist, Orrin Klapp, discusses a southern California gang, the Broadway Riders, in his book, *Collective Search for Identity*, who are poseurs. He writes (1969:103):

> An odd example of group-supported pose is found in a southern California gang called the Broadway Riders—motorcyclists without motorcycles. They affect the style of better-known motorcycle gangs such as the Hell's Angels—black leather jackets, tight pants, boots, long hair, unkempt beards, chains, buckles, sheath knives protruding from boots, slit ear and earring, and so on—but the makeup of this interesting group consists of youths who, for one reason or another...cannot manage to obtain a vehicle. The manager of a motorcycle shop, who knows them well, says: It gives them the position of being tough, to dress like them and be associated with their reputation; yet most aren't really tough at all. They hang around pizza parlors having nothing to do but discuss their exploits and their pseudo-motorcycles.

The Broadway Riders are an excellent example of how people use style to create false identities for themselves—based on psychological phenomena like identification, imitation, and impersonation. But this occurs not only with gangs but with many individuals as well.

Aberrant Decoding

We also have to recognize that the people to whom we send messages about ourselves through our clothes, haircuts, jewelry, and so on, can also not interpret our messages the way we want them to and make mistakes. We can describe this as aberrant decoding.

As an example of this, let me say something about an experiment conducted in a semiotics seminar I taught. My students were asked to bring an object to class in a brown paper bag (so nobody in the class knew who brought which object) that reflected their personality. The students were also asked to leave a list of what they believed the object signified.

Figure 10.3: Seashell

Photo by the author.

The first object taken out was a six-inch seashell. I asked the students to tell me what it signified. They said things like death, emptiness, and sterility. The list my student made read beautiful, natural, lovely, etc. What we learn from this exercise is that people who see us won't necessarily interpret our "looks" the way we think they will.

It is through brands that we purchase that we create a sense of personal identity and become branded selves, but, as was pointed out earlier, it is not only through the brands but through the model or styles of the brands we choose to create a self. We may drive a Mercedes, but is it an entry-level Mercedes, such as an A-Class Sedan ($34,000) or a top-of-the-line Mercedes-Maybach S-Class Sedan ($185,000)?

The Importance of Success

What is important for some people, is the brand (and not the model), and those driving an A-Class Sedan still have the pleasure of seeing that Mercedes Tri-Star on the hood of their car. This, I would suggest, means a great deal to them because driving a Mercedes or its competitors such as Audi and BMW (or any other expensive brand of car) is generally interpreted as signifiers of someone who is a success.

Figure 10.4: Joan Riviere

Joan Riviere, a British psychoanalyst, explains why symbols of success are so important to us. She writes, in *Love, Hate and Reparation* (1964:27):

> Some measure of greed exists unconsciously in everyone. It represents an aspect of the desire to live, one which is mingled and fused at the outset of life with the impulse to turn aggression and destructiveness outside ourselves against others, and as such it persists unconsciously throughout life. By its very nature it is endless and never assuaged; and being a form of the impulse to live, it ceases only with death. The longing or greed for good things can relate to any and every imaginable kind of good—material possessions, bodily or mental gifts, advantages, and privileges; but, besides the actual gratifications they may bring, in the depths of our minds, they ultimately signify one thing. They stand as proofs to us, if we get them, that we are ourselves good, and full of good, and so are worthy of love, or respect and honour, in return. Thus they serve as proofs and insurances against our fears of emptiness inside ourselves, or of our evil impulses which make us feel bad and full of badness to ourselves and others.

It is our taste in the selection of "good things" that plays an important role in our developing a sense of self, in presenting our branded selves to others, and in demonstrating to the world and ourselves that we are worthy of admiration and of love. What I didn't realize when I wrote about the "branded self" is that brands are all expressions of our taste.

Chapter 11

Smartphones

The Oxford dictionary defines a smartphone as a "mobile phone that also has some of the functions of a small computer." That typically means the ability to check your email, browse websites, and use software (like apps for productivity and travel) that require the internet. Where cell phones gave us the ability to call and text without a physical phone line, smartphones provide us with full online access and much richer functionality. The first handheld mobile phone was invented in 1973 by Motorola. The first call was made by Martin Cooper, one of the company's engineers, on a DynaTAC 8000X.

Cell phones became popular in the '90s and early 2000s. As wireless networks improved, especially between 3G and 4G/4G LTE, the technology shifted from cell phones to smartphones. Today, 5G offers even more speed and reliability than ever. Some brands use newer smartphone design to appeal to the nostalgia that many customers have for previously popular cell phones. The Motorola razr, for example, pairs the original foldable form with current-day specs.

The first version of what we'd consider a smartphone was invented in 1992 by IBM. Called the Simon Personal Communicator (or just IBM Simon), it was made available for purchase in 1994 and sold by the tens of thousands. IBM Simon distinguished itself from previous generations of cell phones with features like the ability to send and receive emails, and a touch screen. It also came with built-in programs including:

- Calendar
- Address book
- Appointment scheduler
- Standard and predictive stylus input keyboards
- Electronic notepad
- Handwritten annotations

The design, tools, and performance capabilities of smartphones have evolved massively over the years, however, many of the same features found in the IBM Simon and other early models are now standard in today's smartphones. The term "smartphone" became commonplace as smartphones themselves became more affordable and accessible throughout the 2000s. Many consider the arrival of the first Apple iPhone in 2007 as the first fully realized smartphone. This iconic device allowed for a full internet experience, similar to a laptop or desktop computer. Currently, 85% of adults say they own a smartphone.

https://www.cellularsales.com/blog/a-mostly-quick-history-of-smartphones/

Smartphones have numerous functions, one of which is to display our economic status and technological sophistication. As I pointed out in my *Media Analysis Techniques* 6th Edition (2020:287):

> From a semiotic perspective, the brand and kind of cell phone one purchases offers an opportunity to display one's socioeconomic status, technological savvy, and connoisseurship. The iPhone unleashed an avalanche of smartphones to compete with it. It isn't only the functionality of the iPhone that is important. We also have to consider using an iPhone as a fashion statement and as a signifier that the user is a certain kind of person. Many reviews of cell phones take great pains to describe them in terms of their aesthetics—as art objects and exemplars of great product design.

When people purchase things to show their taste, we can say that these objects are meant for public display. I can recall reading a book about Chinese culture in which the author pointed out that in China people purchase upscale brands for objects that will be seen by others, such as smartphones, automobiles, and watches, and downscale brands for things people will not see, such as refrigerators, washing machines, and stoves. This distinction between private and public probably also applies to people in many other countries.

Figure 11.1: Smartphone with Apps

Drawing by the Author.

Smartphone and Developmental Crises

The brand of cell phone or smartphone one uses can be considered a fashion statement and thus a reflection of one's social status and technological savvy. Smartphones are extremely functional and can play an important role in our lives at every stage of our psychological development. Our phones help us deal with the crises we face and thus are very important to us.

An article in the *PC Magazine Encyclopedia* offers this description of the functionality of smartphones:

> A cellular telephone with built-in applications and Internet access. In addition to digital voice service, modern smartphones provide text messaging, e-mail, Web browsing, still and video cameras, MP3 player, and video playback and calling. In addition to their built-in functions, smartphones run myriad free and paid applications, turning the once single-minded cellphone into a mobile personal computer…In 1994, IBM and BellSouth introduced a combination phone and PDA called the Simon Personal Communicator. Often touted as the first smartphone, Simon was costly and heavy…It took another decade before smartphones became small and powerful enough to be widely used. Introduced in 2002, and due to its focus on e-mail, the BlackBerry became the popular, corporate smartphone, amassing a huge audience over the years. In 2007, the iPhone changed the industry forever.

Since then, Apple has introduced many new models of the iPhone which continues to be the smartphone of choice for billions of people.

This table shows that 1.39 billion smartphones will be shipped in 2022, which reveals that many people continue to purchase new, updated versions of their smartphones, while others who don't have smartphones finally decide to purchase them.

Table 11.1: Sales of Smartphones in 2022. Insiderintelligence.com

Top 5 Smartphone Brands Worldwide, Ranked by Shipments, 2022
millions and % change

1. Samsung	276 (1.1%)
2. Apple	243 (5.4%)
3. Xiaomi	220 (15.8%)
4. Oppo	208 (2.5%)
5. Vivo	149 (6.4%)

Note: total 2022 shipments=1.39 billion
Source: TrendForce as cited in press release, Nov 17, 2021

271500   InsiderIntelligence.com

The Impact of the iPhone

David Brooks wrote an article in the August 7, 2008 *New York Times*, "Lord of the Memes," that deals with the impact of the iPhone, which was introduced to the world on June 29, 2007. He writes:

> On or about June 29, 2007, human character changed…. That, of course, was the release date of the first iPhone.

On that date, Brooks suggests, "media displaced culture," by which he meant that the way we transmitted things, using media, replaced the content of what we create, culture.

There were, according to an article on the Internet by Quentin Hardy that appeared on the *New York Times* "Bits" column (March 27, 2014), "Smartphones, The Disappointing Miracle," 2582 models of smartphones, 691 carriers of mobile messages, 106 operating systems, and around two million apps. That was in 2014. We have to make a distinction between smartphones and mobile phones (cell phones).

On the Internet recently an article saying that there are now 20,000 kinds of Android (non-Apple) phones and tablets which gives us an idea of how much competition there is for smartphones and other kinds of phones.

Bankmycell.com offers the following statistics about smartphone and mobile phone use:

How Many People Have Smartphones In The World?

According to Statista, the current number of smartphone users in the world today is 6.648 billion, and this means 83.96% of the world's population owns a smartphone (as of October 2022). This figure is up considerably from 2016 when there were only 3.668 billion users, 49.40% of that year's global population.

How Many People Have Mobile Phones In The World?

7.26 Billion mobile phone users in the world today 91.69% of people own mobile phones today

In 2022, including both smart and feature phones—that is, cell phones-- the current number of mobile phone users is 7.26 billion, which makes 91.69% of people in the world cell phone owners. Feature phones are the basic cell phones without apps and complex OS systems, more prominent in developing countries.

https://www.bankmycell.com/blog/how-many-phones-are-in-the-world

In short, almost everyone in the world has a smartphone or a cell phone—that is a phone without smartphone features. There are also a bewildering number of choices we can make when it comes to choosing what brand to purchase and then deciding what apps to use on them.

According to Assurion.com, Americans check their phones every ten minutes or 96 times a day. I would describe this as an example of hypervigilance, based on what we may call "Fear of Missing Out." This continually checking is based upon our anxieties about opportunities we may be missing or anxieties we might harbor about things that may happen to us.

Smartphone Addiction

The functionality and ease of smartphone use may also be the source of behavior we can describe as addictive. A *PLOS ONE* article, "The Smartphone Addiction Scale: Development and Validation of a Short Version for Adolescents" by Min Kwon, Dai-Jin Kim, Hyun Cho, and Soo Yang discusses this topic (Published: December 31, 2013, https://doi.org/10.1371/journal.pone.0083558):

> Considering its mobile and internet capabilities, a smartphone also has the possibility of becoming a prevalent social problem as it signifies the characteristics of addiction such as tolerance, withdrawal, difficulty in performing daily activities, or impulse control disorders as confirmed in previous studies. Kuss & Griffiths have mentioned the possibility of a social networking sites (SNS) addiction through their online social networking study and Park & Lee also reported that smartphone use could be attributed to loneliness, depression, and self-esteem based on their smartphone use and psychological well-being study.

One of the reasons for this unexpected popularity of smartphones is that it makes people's lives more convenient. However, this may also pose many risks for such dependence on a gadget. This 'smartphone addiction' recently has become an important issue in our society. According to the study related to the development of smartphone addiction scale, smartphones also caused symptoms of addiction similar to the effects of the internet including craving, withdrawal, tolerance, daily-life disturbance, and preference of cyberspace-oriented relationships, which were confirmed through the diagnosis. We have a situation with smartphones and other devices where their functionality ultimately turns out to be dysfunctional since their hyper-functionality often leads to addictive behavior.

An article in *The Guardian* suggests that many children have "problematic cell phone use:"

> One in four children and young people could have problematic smartphone use, according to research that also suggests such behaviour is associated with poorer mental health. The amount of time children and teens spend using their devices has become an issue of

growing concern, but experts say there is still little evidence as to whether spending time on screens is harmful in itself.

https://www.theguardian.com/society/2019/nov/29/one-in-four-children-have-problematic-smartphone-use

The smartphone has had an amazing impact on everyone's life. With a smartphone, everyone is now a potential photojournalist, and videos taken by people with smartphones have been important in showing police violence. A video taken by a bystander while George Floyd was killed by a policeman, Derek Chauvin, kneeling on his throat, led to his being convicted of murder.

It is possible to make a film using a smartphone and several films have been made using iPhones and other smartphones. Since there are millions of applications available for smartphones (2.2 million for the iPhone) it means these devices can do an incredible number of things. The question we face when thinking about people and their smartphones is: who will be the master?

Chapter 12

Men's Facial Hair

A beard has both social and political meanings. "A powerful distinguishing mark, the appearance of facial hair plays a key role in the process of asserting or stigmatising identity," says ethnologist Christian Bromberger. "Being hairless and clean-shaven, or not, is far from neutral," says Stéphane Héas, a sociologist at Rennes 2 University. "One's appearance impacts directly on the way others judge us."

Beards often have political connotations. The pharaohs wore fake beards, not to accentuate their wisdom, but because the beards were seen as a divine attribute, "a symbol of power."

"The patriarchal, male-dominant nature of western society in the 19th and 20th century almost certainly explains the appeal of sophisticated beards and moustaches," Héas writes. "Policymakers made their presence felt through their discourse and facial hair."

Beards may have social connotations, too. "An unruly beard, if combined with other factors – threadbare clothes and a generally poor physical state – suggests someone who is poor, underprivileged, maybe even homeless, unlike a person with a neatly trimmed beard, which means they can afford this type of attention," says Marie-Hélène Delavaud-Roux, joint editor of *Anthropologie, Mythologies et Histoire de la Chevelure*, a collective work on hair and beards. "When styled and domesticated a beard is no longer symptomatic of poor hygiene."

But each epoch gives rise to particular practices. "Social norms determine how far a beard should be allowed to grow, when it should be trimmed or shaved off," Héas points out. You can see at a glance the difference between a photograph of a belle époque politician and a bearded socialist of the 1980s. And the norms keep changing.

https://www.bing.com/search?q=sociology+of+beards&cvid=ff4eaf1ff4 ea4cf8abb1956ce86fd2af&aqs=edge.0.69i59i450l8...8.1047917009j0j4& FORM=ANAB01&PC=ACTS

In the past few years or so, beards have become increasingly popular. You see beards on baseball players, football players, executives in organizations, and many other men. On the Internet, there is a site that says the beards started becoming popular around 2005, but doesn't explain why they became popular.

Facial Hair and Fashion

At the same time that men started allowing the hair underneath their noses and on their chins to start growing longer, we find many men, especially balding men, shaving off all the hair on the top of their heads. Both of these phenomena are ways in which men demonstrate their sense of style and are reflections of personal taste and the power of fashion, which is a social force. This photo of Blaine Reeves shows the power of style in his Dali-like mustache and long beard.

Figure 12.1: Blaine Reeves

Used by permission of Blaine Reeves.

In her book, *Dress Codes: Meanings and Messages in American Culture,* sociologist Ruth Rubinstein discusses religious injunctions about beards (1995:86):

Clement of Alexandria, a church father of the first century A.D. declared that beards were a badge of masculinity and that it was sacrilegious to trifle with them because they were a symbol of man's stronger nature. He claimed that "by God's decree hairiness is one of man's conspicuous qualities....Whatever smoothness or softness there was in him God took from him when he fashioned the delicate Eve from his side...his characteristic is action; hers, passivity."

Later in the book, in a discussion of the "Legitimacy of the Individuated Self," she explains (1995:242):

> Courts in recent years have supported the distinction between the public and the personal self. Judges have ruled in favor of school boards trying to implement dress codes for teachers, but they have distinguished between work attire and an individual's choice of personal appearance. They have maintained that long hair, a beard, or a moustache is an aspect of a teacher's personal self. To try to regulate these elements of appearance represents a violation of individual rights.

She then discusses a case in which the Massachusetts State Police tried to get six members of the police force to shave off their mustaches. As she writes (1995:242-243):

> Not only for police but for all men facial hair alters the individual's appearance and how he is perceived by others. Such alteration can be cosmetic such as growing a beard to cover up a weak chin or jowl or growing a mustache to provide a horizontal element in a long, angular face, as noted in *Man at His Best: Esquire's Guide to Style*. A beard can also be a political statement, as it was for many activists in the late 1960s."

Wearing a mustache or a beard, or both is a fashion statement and should be seen as a kind of messaging men provide for others. Fashion is a collective force and many men who have mustaches or beards or shaved heads are likely going along with fashion rather than thinking about what kind of messages they are sending to others about themselves.

A Brief Case Study About a Very Short Beard

Below is a brief case study involving an 83-year-old friend of mine who mentioned in an email that he had just shaved off his beard. I wrote and asked him a few questions, which he answered as follows.

1. Why did you decide to wear a beard? What turned you on to a beard?

I guess it was because a lot of friends had beards.

2. Why did you decide to wear the style of beard you chose?

I really don't recall, perhaps because decades ago, I had a full beard and didn't like it.

3. Why did you decide to shave off your beard?

This is the only one I can really answer. As a celebration of Trump losing.

PS. I left the mustache.

One thing we learned from this brief exchange is that my friend grew a beard because his friends had beards and so he was "going along" with fashion. His beard was a goatee and neither my wife nor I thought it was attractive. He thought it was a fashion statement.

We can learn more about fashion, not only about fashion in facial hair but about fashion in general, from Georg Simmel, a German sociologist who had interesting things to say about many topics.

Figure 12.2: Georg Simmel

SIMMEL

Georg Simmel on Fashion

Georg Simmel (1858-1918) discussed fashion and its role in society in an essay titled "The Philosophy of Fashion," in which he offered some important insights (in David Frisby and Mike Featherstone (Eds.), *Simmel on Culture* (1997:192):

> The essence of fashion consists of the fact that it should always be exercised by only part of a given group, the great majority of whom are merely on the road to adopting it. As soon as fashion has been universally adopted, that is, as soon as anything that was originally done only by a few has really come to be practiced by all—as is the case in certain elements of clothing and various forms of social conduct—we no longer characterize it as fashion. Every growth of fashion drives it to its doom, because it thereby cancels out its distinctiveness....Fashion's question is not that of being, but rather it is simultaneously being and non-being; it always stands on the watershed of the past and the future and, as a result, conveys to us, at least while it is at its height, a stronger sense of the present than do most other phenomena.

What we learn from Simmel is that fashion is always in flux, always evolving, but once a fashion is accepted by large numbers of people, it loses its power to differentiate fashionable people from others. Thus, it must be replaced, so fashions are continually being born and discarded. Some people, who are not fashionable, adopt the latest fashions because they are envious of those who are fashionable or because they don't wish to be noticed. Being fashionable is a way for many people to escape notice.

From a semiotic perspective, clothes, objects, and facial hair are signs that convey information about fashionable people. In *Dress Codes: Meanings and Messages in American Culture,* Ruth P. Rubinstein writes (1995:3):

> Most social scientists take it for granted that an individual's clothing expresses meaning. They accept the old saw that "a picture is worth a thousand words" and generally concede that dress and ornament are elements in a communication system. They recognize that a person's attire can indicate either conformity or resistance to socially defined expectations for behavior. Yet few scholars have attempted to explain the meaning and relevance of clothing systematically. They often mistake it for *fashion* (in a person's desired appearance) whereas *clothing* refers to established patterns of dress. As a result, neither clothing images nor the rules that govern their use have been adequately identified or explained.

What Rubinstein writes about clothing can be applied to men's facial hair: beards, mustaches, and shaved heads are messages people send to others about themselves. These messages are shaped by the social force we know as fashion and thus as fashion changes, so do things like wearing a mustache or beard (or both) and shaving one's head.

I should add that people don't just wear a mustache, but a particular kind of mustache. If you examine photographs of men with mustaches, you find many variations in the style of mustaches. For example, Salvador Dali, a surrealist artist, had a very distinctive mustache. He was known for his waxed mustache, which he styled into two thin, upward-pointing curves.

Styles of Mustaches

An article on the Internet on Beardbrand.com deals with mustaches:

> It's 2021, mustaches are back in style, and as always, people are divided. "The world needs to face a cold hard truth, 99% of mustaches don't look good," writes Benjamin Davis. It's a satirical piece, but in the article's comments section, a woman named Kristen chimes in: "Mustaches don't look good on anyone. Just ewww!" Another woman named Carol writes, "Thank you, thank you. I hate mustaches." 95 people have applauded (the equivalent of a Reddit upvote) Carol's comment. Disdain for mustaches isn't a new response or a lazy indictment of a style that has long been dormant from the public eye. It's a story that has played out

time and time again, even at the height of mustache popularity. 41 years ago, Freddie Mercury's mustache made its first appearance. Now known as the chevron mustache, it's become one of the most iconic 'stache styles of all time.

https://www.beardbrand.com/blogs/urbanbeardsman/mustaches

Dapper Confidential on the Internet offers this note on trends in beards:

> Beards have long been a classic look for men and realistically, they won't be disappearing anytime soon. Some trend-followers who jumped on the bandwagon might decide to shave however, we don't expect that everyone will. Many guys, including some bearded celebrities, learned the joys of facial hair and not-shaving and we don't expect them to abandon their beards and go for the no-beard look. That said, the scruffy lumberjack look seems to be evolving into a better-maintained, more professional, and shaped beard. Men will be looking for ways to cultivate a polished beard, looking for better trimming methods as well as tools to tame their facial hair.
>
> The most attractive style in 2022 would undoubtedly be a clean and tidy beard. With many in the workplace being required to wear facial masks and PPE gear on their face, the hipster 1800's beards of yesteryear are definitely OUT! I believe that beards will definitely still hold their own in 2022. Although, I suspect that in general, the length size will come down and popular beards will be those close to the face and short in length.

https://www.dapperconfidential.com/beards-vs-clean-shaven-whats-hot/

What we learn from Dapper Confidential is that some people who wear beards are "trend-followers" and wear beards because they are seen as fashionable. Dapper Confidential also offers advice about the kind of beards that are seen as attractive and those that are unfashionable and OUT! Hipster beards may be out, as far as Dapper Confidential is concerned, but quite a few men wear them.

Figure 12.3: Michel Foucault

Drawing by the author.

Shaved Heads

Vogue magazine provides some historical background and insights into shaved heads:

> As the '60s began, skinheads emerged as a new youth subculture in east London and the shaved head was embraced as a bold and defiant look. These working-class groups donned combat boots and bomber jackets, their identity shaped by their opposition to middle-class 'longhairs' (or hippies). To some, this tribe's look was menacing, and became increasingly so years later when it was co-opted by racists and neo-Nazis. Ironically, the initial subculture surfaced as a non-racist, multiracial scene, having grown out of reggae and ska music....In later musical subcultures, the shaved head became a mainstay. Kathleen Hanna, the pioneer of feminist punk movement 'riot grrrl' in the early '90s, reportedly had a shaved head — which makes complete sense for a group that raised a middle finger to cultural conservatives and gender stereotypes.
>
> https://www.vogue.co.uk/beauty/article/significance-of-shaved-heads

What we learn from this *Vogue* article is that shaved heads, like so many other aspects of fashion, emerged from working-class subcultures and had a social and political dimension. Women who were Nazi sympathizers had their heads shaved after the Second World War and shaved heads can be found in films and fashion photographs for many years.

Two Hypothesis on Facial Hair

A hypothesis can be defined as an informed guess, a suggestion that explains something but one that is not based on experiments, a supposition, or a proposed explanation based on limited evidence as a starting point for further investigation.

Hypothesis 1: Beards and Feminism

Let me offer a hypothesis on beards and mustaches. We can regard them as signifiers of hyper-masculinity and their popularity may be seen as a reaction, on the part of men, to the increased assertiveness of women and their gaining positions of power in the business world and politics. Beards and mustaches, then, are unconscious reactions by men who feel threatened by the new assertiveness of women and so beards and mustaches are a kind of nostalgic regression to earlier periods when women "knew their place" and men were dominant.

Hypothesis 2: Semantic Self-Delusions About The Tops of Men's Heads

Generally, we think of men who are bald as having hair with patches of their scalp showing through. If that is the case, what can we say about men who shave their heads so there are no bald spots and who are thus disguising their balding. Perhaps we can distinguish between bald and hairless with hairless men seeing themselves as not bald but with shaved heads. Bald is generally defined as having wholly or partly lacking hair, but I think in common usage, we usually mean the second part of that definition—partly lacking hair. If a man has a full head of hair and shaves it all off, then we can define that as a pure fashion statement.

One thing about fashion is that tastes change and so it is conceivable that in a few years or a few decades, people's attitudes towards their facial hair will change and mustaches and beards will lose their popularity and will be replaced by a "clean" look—without mustaches and beards and shaved heads in most men or with combinations that will emerge from some subculture somewhere that becomes fashionable.

Chapter 13

Bad Taste Jokes

There are as many different functions and styles of humor as there are versions of the old joke, "How many ____ does it take to change a light bulb?" So why do we crack up at some jokes while others fall flat? Scientists have proposed competing explanations for why some things are funnier than others, but it seems clear that humor often involves the violation of expectations. Culture, age, political orientation, and many other factors likely also play a role in what people find funny.

What makes something funny? Some who have sought to explain humor point to the fact that many jokes or funny events contradict one's sense of how things are supposed to be. The theory of benign violations proposes that something is funny when it seems both wrong or threatening *and* essentially harmless—as when a comedian says something shocking but clearly unserious. (What counts as benign depends on the perceiver of the joke.) Other theories of what makes things funny focus on the role of tension-relief, suddenly "getting" how incongruous details fit together, and other factors.

Why are some people funnier than others?
In addition to being skilled in toying with people's expectations, people who are funnier than most may exhibit qualities such as a willingness to take risks when making jokes and a sensitivity to how their attempts at humor are perceived. More gifted comedians might also be more intelligent, on average.

Not everyone can be a great comedian, but many of us are the jokester of the family, the class clown, or the funniest friend in the group. Given the appeal of a quick wit and a robust sense of humor, it's natural to wonder whether you are among the funny ones—and whether there are ways to become funnier.

https://www.psychologytoday.com/us/basics/humor

Most of the time we laugh at things that happen in our everyday lives-- mistakes people make, comic insults, misunderstandings, revelations of ignorance or stupidity, and so on, rather than jokes.

What is a Joke?

Jokes, technically speaking, can be defined as short narratives, meant to amuse and generate mirthful laughter, that end with a punch line. In the case of shaggy dog stories, the narratives can be relatively long, but as a rule, jokes are rather short texts.

Many people think the way to be funny and gain the benefits derived from being amusing is to tell jokes. This is a bad idea for three reasons.

1. *The joke may be lousy.* If you tell a joke that isn't funny, you'll mildly antagonize people who expect to be entertained and amused.

2. *You may not tell jokes well.* Even if you have a good joke, if you don't tell it well, people won't be amused.

3. *Your listener(s) may have already heard the joke.* This forces people to pretend to be amused and fake laughter, which can be quite painful for them.

Two questions suggest themselves now. First, how can you be funny without telling jokes, and second, what makes a joke funny—that is, how do jokes work? My answer to these questions is that we should use the techniques of humor found in jokes to create our own humor, based on our personalities, our comedic tendencies, and that sort of thing. This topic will be discussed shortly.

As explained earlier, a joke is a particular form of humor and they are one of the most commonly used forms of humor. What humor is has interested many of our greatest minds, from Aristotle's time to the present.

The Structure of a Joke

The linear structure of a joke is shown in the diagram below:

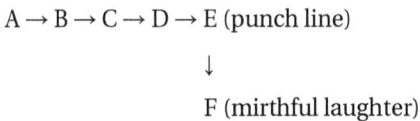

A → B → C → D → E (punch line)

↓

F (mirthful laughter)

A through E are the set-up parts of the joke, E represents the punch line, and F represents mirthful laughter. I offer a joke below with its parts given letters.

A. Someone calls Radio Erevan in Soviet Armenia and asks, "Is it true that Comrade Gorshenko won 5,000 rubles?

B. Radio Erevan answers, "Yes, that is correct."

C. "But it was not Comrade Gorshenko but Comrade Gatov."

D. "And was not 5,000 rubles but 10,000 rubles."

> E. "And he didn't win it but lost it, gambling. (PUNCH LINE)
>
> F. Mirthful laughter.

There are many other forms of humor, such as puns and witty remarks, but if a text is to be a joke, it must be a narrative and have a punch line.

Bad taste in jokes describes ones that are inappropriate, unpleasant, insulting, and disturbing. Jokes are texts that are told by someone to someone else—often preceded by a statement such as "Have you heard this one?" and exist in a play frame that gives the joke teller a certain amount of latitude as far as good taste is concerned.

The play frame means, "this is not serious." But in many cases, the joke teller breaches the norms of good taste and propriety causing problems for the joke teller, such as the exposure of ignorance, insensitivity, racist beliefs, anti-Semitic beliefs, sexist beliefs, etc., and general lack of good sense.

Jokes can also cause problems for those who are told the joke, such as embarrassment and estrangement from the joke teller.

Three dominant theories of humor

There are three basic theories that explain why we laugh: superiority theory, psychoanalytic (release) theories, and incongruity theories.

Aristotle and Hobbes, two superiority theorists, suggest that humor involves lowly types, people made ridiculous or, as Hobbes put it in his classic statement, humor involves a "sudden glory arising from some sudden conception of some eminency in ourselves; by comparison with the infirmity of others, or with our own formerly." (Piddington 1963, 160) Our laughter is based on our feeling of being superior to someone or something in some respect.

The psychoanalytic (release) theorists deal with humor and the psyche and, as explained by Freud in his book, *Jokes and Their Relation to the Unconscious* (1963), involves the unconscious, masked aggression, and various intrapsychic economies that humor provides. We can enjoy the aggression and comedic hostility found in comedians without a sense of guilt.

Incongruity theorists argue (and it is the most widely held theory of humor) argue that namely that there is a difference between what we expect and what we get in jokes and other forms of humor. Thus, the philosopher Schopenhauer suggested that we laugh at the "...sudden perception of the incongruity between a concept and the real objects which have been thought through it in some relation, and laughter itself is just the expression of this incongruity." (Piddington 1963: 171-172)

These theories tell us why people laugh, in general, but they cannot explain what it is that makes people laugh at a joke or a line in a play or any humorous text other than in very general terms. I call them "why" theories of humor. Why theories, from my perspective, operate at too high a level of abstraction and don't really explain what it is in a given text that generates the desired goal of amusement or mirthful laughter.

The Forty-Five Techniques of Humor

To determine in a more granular way what makes people laugh, I did some research, and I discovered forty-five techniques of humor that fall into four categories: language, logic, identity, and visual phenomena or action. These techniques, in combination with one another (and in some cases when reversed), can help us find, with more precision than was possible before, what it is that generates humor in texts.

These techniques can be classified as the humor of language, logic, identity, and action.

Table 13.1: 45 Techniques of Humor by Category

LANGUAGE	LOGIC	IDENTITY	ACTION
Allusion	Absurdity	Before/After	Chase
Bombast	Accident	Burlesque	Slapstick
Definition	Analogy	Caricature	Speed
Exaggeration	Catalogue	Eccentricity	
Facetiousness	Coincidence	Embarrassment	
Insults	Comparison	Exposure	
Infantilism	Disappointment	Grotesque	
Irony	Ignorance	Imitation	
Misunderstanding	Mistakes	Impersonation	
Over literalness	Repetition	Mimicry	
Puns/Wordplay	Reversal	Parody	
Repartee	Rigidity	Scale	
Ridicule	Theme & Var.	Stereotype	
Sarcasm	Satire	Unmasking	

45 TECHNIQUES OF HUMOR BY CATEGORY

1. Absurdity	16. Embarrassment	31. Parody
2. Accident	17. Exaggeration	32. Puns
3. Allusion	18. Exposure	33. Repartee
4. Analogy	19. Facetiousness	34. Repetition
5. Before/After	20. Grotesque	35. Reversal
6. Bombast	21. Ignorance	36. Ridicule
7. Burlesque	22. Imitation	37. Rigidity
8. Caricature	23. Impersonation	38. Sarcasm
9. Catalogue	24. Infantilism	39. Satire
10. Chase Scene	25. Insults	40. Scale, Size

11. Coincidence	26. Irony	41. Slapstick
12. Comparison	27. Literalness	42. Speed
13. Definition	28. Mimicry	43. Stereotypes
14. Disappointment	29. Mistakes	44. Theme/Variation
15. Eccentricity	30. Misunderstanding	45. Unmasking

45 Techniques of Humor in Alphabetical Order

To make it easier to use of this list of techniques, they've been numbered and listed in alphabetical order. With this list of techniques, it is possible to deconstruct a joke by listing the techniques that are found generating the humor in that joke—or, by extension, any other humorous form such as a humorous play or film.

This typology of the forty-five techniques of humor was used in a book I wrote on dramatic comedies, which was reviewed by a linguistics scholar, Don L. F. Nilsen, who suggested my typology of 45 techniques of humor is an important contribution to the study of humor. He writes, in a review of my book, *The Art of Comedy Writing*, which appeared in *Humor: The International Journal of Humor Research* (*Humor, 12-1*, 1999:96-97):

> For the work that I am presently doing involving humor in British, American, and Irish literature, Arthur Asa Berger has provided a very insightful and useful methodology for analyzing and creating humorous discourse in his *The Art of Comedy Writing*. For me, his model is as powerful as such other discourse models as "Script Model Grammar," by Raskin and others, "Conversational Implicatures," by Grice and others, "Conversational Analysis," by Tannen and others, "Genre and Archetype Theory," by Frye, White, and others, "Signification Theory," by Henry Lewis Gates and others, "Dialogique Theory," by Bakhtin and others, various ethnographic and linguistic models by Schiffrin and others, or indeed any discourse model I have studied and/or used. Although Berger's model is flawed in many ways, and although it is presented in a glib fashion, it is nevertheless a powerful and rigorous model. Its power comes from its detail (45 techniques of devices) and its rigor comes from how this detail is spelled out (15 "Language" devices, 14 "Logic" devices, 13 "Identity" devices, and 3 "Action" devices.

His reviews suggest that my model is of some consequence in the scholarly study of humor and is as powerful as other models used in the study of humor.

An Application of the Techniques of Humor to a Joke

Below is an example of how these techniques can be used to analyze a joke, and a list of the techniques used in the joke to generate mirthful laughter.

The Tan

A man goes to Miami for a vacation. After four days, he notices he has a tan all over his body, except for his penis. So the next day, he goes to a deserted area of the beach early in the morning, takes his clothes off, and lies down. He sprinkles sand over himself until all that remains in the sun is his penis. Two little old ladies walk by on the boardwalk and one notices the penis. "When I was 20," she says, "I was scared to death of them. When I was 40, I couldn't get enough of them. When I was 60, I couldn't get one to come near me….and now they're growing wild on the beach."

In this joke, we have a few techniques at work.

15, Eccentricity.

The man must have every bit of his body tanned, even his penis.

29, Mistakes.

The old lady thinks that penises are growing wild on the beach.

18, Exposure.

The exhibitionism of the man and the sexual desire of the woman.

There generally is a dominant technique and then one or more secondary techniques in jokes. What this exercise demonstrates is that jokes are more complicated than we might imagine. Jokes also can be dangerous as many politicians discover, to their dismay, when they try to be funny and end up insulting people and making fools of themselves. This leads to my next topic, bad taste in jokes.

Bad Taste in Jokes

There are, on the Internet, many lists of "bad taste" jokes which reveal that bad taste in jokes is a common phenomenon. We might ask, what is it in a joke that makes it in bad taste? Let me offer some suggestions.

1. Individual insult jokes.

These jokes insult individuals and attack their looks, their beliefs, their ideas, their politics, or some other attribute.

2. Group insult jokes

These jokes insult groups of people because of their race, religion, gender, politics, ethnicity, nationality, and other social characteristics. We also have to consider the level of hostility found in the joke. Some "insults" are broad and poke fun at people or nationalities, while others can be extremely hostile and even vicious.

Al Gini writes, in the *Florida Philosophical Review* Volume XV, Issue 1, Winter 2015, about "Dirty Jokes, Tasteless, Jokes, Ethnic Jokes" and explains:

> The simple fact is every utterance has the potential to offend. "Writing or speaking humorously is like playing with matches; it can burn the one who's trying to light up the darkness." The issue I am pursuing here is not whether a joke is ethically correct or ethically objectionable. Rather, the issue is, how is it possible that an utterly tasteless joke, a joke that many consider to be crude, rude, inappropriate, highly offensive, and even harmful be considered to be funny?.... Ted Cohen argues that all jokes are conditional. That is, all jokes have conditional requirements connecting the teller and the audience, i.e., common knowledge, common background, common language, common cultural presuppositions, prejudices, and myths.

Gini raises the question of how a joke can be insulting, hateful, nasty, in bad taste, and still be funny. My answer would be that our response to jokes, that is, to their punch lines, is involuntary, so a bad-taste joke, whatever else it might be, still can be very funny. We are responding to the joke even though it is in bad taste because of the gratification and pleasure the joke provides.

People who tell jokes of bad taste can be seen as anomic—not obeying the norms of society. In some cases, people who tell these jokes may not be aware of what they are doing but in many cases, as in anti-Black jokes, anti-Catholic jokes, anti-Semitic jokes, and sexist jokes, the joke tellers know what they are doing and do so because of their need to communicate their feelings of superiority (as Aristotle would put it) about the members of the groups who are attacked or ridiculed.

Chapter 14

Popular Fiction: Mysteries

Detective story, type of popular literature in which a crime is introduced and investigated and the culprit is revealed.

The traditional elements of the detective story are: (1) the seemingly perfect crime; (2) the wrongly accused suspect to whom circumstantial evidence points; (3) the bungling of dim-witted police; (4) the greater powers of observation and superior mind of the detective; and (5) the startling and unexpected denouement, in which the detective reveals how the identity of the culprit was ascertained. Detective stories frequently operate on the principle that superficially convincing evidence is ultimately irrelevant. Usually, it is also axiomatic that the clues from which a logical solution to the problem can be reached be fairly presented to the reader at exactly the same time that the sleuth receives them and that the sleuth deduce the solution to the puzzle from a logical interpretation of these clues.

https://www.britannica.com/art/detective-story-narrative-genre

Crime fiction, by definition, deals in the impermissible, in the ethical boundaries society has set down and the consequences of crossing them—and also to some extent, considers whether these are the right lines to draw. As such, crime stories provide a powerful and enduringly relevant lens through which to examine human behavior and motivation, interpersonal relationships, and the structures and systems which keep us in place. Perhaps this is the reason for readers' ongoing fascination with mystery and crime, through all its incarnations.

Jane Pek, Review of *Elementary. The New York Times Book Review*, September 11, 2022. Page 19.

We can distinguish between "elite" novels, which can take many forms, and popular fiction genres, such as mysteries, romances, science-fiction, and horror stories, which are formulaic. James Joyce's *Finnegan's Wake* and *Ulysses* are exemplars of "elite" novels and require a certain amount of education and sophistication to be able to read and appreciate them.

This chapter will deal with an important genre of popular fiction, mystery novels. We learn from examining mysteries that, although they are formulaic, there is ample room in the mystery formula for innovation and creativity.

There are three basic categories of mysteries:

Classical detective: Novels by Agatha Christie
Tough guy detective: Novels by Dashiell Hammett
Police procedural: Novels by Michael Connolly

Formulas

John Cawelti, author of *The Six-Gun Mystique,* discusses the nature of formulas: (1971, 27)

> All cultural products contain a mixture of two elements: conventions and inventions. Conventions are elements that are known to both the creator and his audience beforehand--they consist of things like favorite plots, stereotyped characters, accepted ideas, commonly known metaphors, other linguistic devices, etc. Inventions, on the other hand, are elements that are uniquely imagined by the creator such as new kinds of characters, ideas, or linguistic forms.

What we find is that there is plenty of room within formulas for writers to evade the "restrictions" in formulaic works and establish an identity and style that people like.

Genres

A genre is a kind of popular fiction that has formulaic aspects. When we watch television, go to the movies, read a book, or wander around the Internet, the texts we choose are generally based on our like or dislike of certain genres, a French term that means "kind." or "category." People essentially decide what genres they like and what texts in those genres to read or watch.

As Douglas Kellner explains in Television Images, *Codes and Messages* (1980: Vol. 7, No. 4):

> A genre consists of a coded set of formulas and conventions which indicate a culturally accepted way of organizing material into distinct patterns. Once established, genres dictate the basic conditions of cultural production and reception. For example, crime dramas invariably have a violent crime, a search for its perpetrators, and often a chase, fight, or bloody elimination of the criminal, communicating the message "crime does not pay." The audience comes to expect these predictable pleasures and a crime drama "code" develops, enshrined in production and studio texts and practices.

To make things more complicated, many genres have sub-genres. Thus, for example, the detective genre has three sub-genres: the classical detective story with a detective who uses his or her brains (Sherlock Holmes), the tough guy detective story with a hero who is smart but also who is good with his fists (Sam Spade), and the procedural detective story (CSI) about police laboratories and teams of police fighting crime.

A search on Google (accessed 11/1/2021) reveals that the most popular fiction genres are:

1. *Romance/Erotica--$1.44 billion*—From the success of the Fifty Shades of Grey trilogy and the number of novels written by people like Danielle Steel, there's no surprise that romance and erotica are #1.

2. *Crime/Mystery—$728.2 million*—There's nothing like the thrill from a mystery novel. The suspense is intriguing enough that it keeps you on board. It's all about the build-up, the surprises, even the letdowns. Crime and mystery stories are so wild and fascinating, but also seem plausible.

3. *Religious/Inspirational—$720 million*—Things may be going great but you may need a little push. Everyone can use some inspiration. From how-to books, holy texts, and even memoirs, inspirational and religious texts.

4. *Science Fiction/Fantasy—$590.2 million*—Dragons, elves, witches, robots, the possibilities are endless. We love escaping into a fictional land. There's nothing that people can't achieve through magic or extraordinary circumstances in this genre.

5. *Horror—$79.6 million*—Horror has earned its place on this list. If you think of Stephen King and the ways his work has been adapted to screen, or old horrors like Dracula and Frankenstein, there are endless stories that people love.

https://bookadreport.com/book-market-overview-authors-statistics-facts/

Mysteries, we see, are the second most popular genre. We can compare the formulas for different genres and see how they differ. I created this chart to show the more important aspects of three popular fiction genres.

Table 14.1: Formulas in Popular Fiction Genres

Genre	Mystery	Western	Science-Fiction
Time	Present (but anytime is okay)	The 1800s	Future
Location	Cities	Edge of Civilization	Outer Space
Hero	Detective	Cowboy	Space Man
Heroine	Damsel in Distress	Schoolmarm	Space Gal
Secondary	Friends of Heroine	Town people Indians	Technicians
Villains	Murderers, Criminals	Outlaws	Aliens
Plot	Find Villain	Restore Law and Order	Repel Aliens
Theme	Justice will prevail	Justice and Progress	Save Humanity
Costume	Suits, Dresses	Cowboy Hat	Space Gear
Locomotion	Automobiles	Horse	Rocket Ship
Weaponry	Guns, Fists	Six-Gun	Ray Gun Laser Gun

Narratives

A narrative is a story and a story, in essence, is a sequence of events, which means that narratives tend to take place within a certain period. They tend to be linear, but in some cases, narratives jump around and move in various configurations.

A Russian literary scholar, Yuri Lotman, has argued in *The Structure of the Artistic Text* that everything in a text is significant. As he explained (1997:17):

> The tendency to interpret everything in an artistic text as meaningful is so great that we rightfully consider nothing accidental in a work of art.

This means that everything plays a role in narratives, even though something said or a description may seem irrelevant at first sight. Stories all have gaps in them and are full of holes since writers can't describe every thought and every idea a character might have and everything characters do. So it is the role of readers to fill in the gaps and make sense of things as best they can. This means that readers play an important role in interpreting what a story is all about.

Readers of stories are always absorbing a lot of information and trying to figure out what it all adds up to. We are so used to this behavior that we take little notice of it, but writers are aware of this process and provide an enormous amount of information in the devices such as dialogue and description.

Wolfgang Iser, a German professor, wrote an article about what he called "the role of the reader," in which he argued that it takes readers to bring a book into being. So it is the potential readers of the book that make it come into being (when they read the book) and this shapes the way the writers tell their stories.

Writers always have certain audiences in mind, which affects the way they write their stories and the kinds of stories they write. Writers use various techniques to tell their stories. One way writers inform readers about what is going on in a story is through dialogue in which characters speak to one another. This dialogue enables writers to provide information about the backgrounds of characters, their personalities, their motivations, their beliefs, their values, and countless other things.

Often characters reveal things about themselves unconsciously—things they try to keep hidden. So readers are always scrutinizing dialogue in an attempt to figure out what role these characters will play in the story. The dialogue of the main characters is important but so is the dialogue among secondary characters. The language used in dialogue reveals a great deal about speakers. We have to recognize that every word a writer uses represents a choice and is intended to convey a certain meaning. Sometimes, overheard conversations play a role in stories. These conversations and descriptions are the way authors convey important information to readers.

What follows is an example of dialogue from Dashiell Hammett's *The Maltese Falcon.*

> The door opened and Iva Archer came in. She said, "Hello, honey," in a voice as lightly amiable as his face had suddenly become...
>
> "Oh, Sam, forgive me! forgive me!" she cried in a choked voice.

> She stood just inside the door, wadding black-bordered handkerchief in her small gloved hands, peering into his face with frightened red and swollen eyes. He did not get up from his seat on the desk-corner.
>
> He said: "Sure. That's all right. Forget it."
>
> "But, Sam," she wailed, "I sent those policemen there. I was mad, crazy with jealousy, and I phoned them that if they'd go there, they'd learn something about Mile's murder."
>
> "What made you think that?"
>
> "Oh, I didn't! But I was mad, Sam, and I wanted to hurt you." "It made things damned awkward." He put his arm around her and drew her nearer. "But it's all right now, only don't get any more crazy notions like that."

When writers describe people or things, they use these descriptions to provide readers with information that often is of vital importance. Writers can hide clues to a crime or the motivation of their characters in their descriptions. Readers learn to search for information in descriptions that will help them anticipate how a story might be resolved. We have to recognize that an author can spend a thousand words describing a character and readers still don't know what they look like. But they can imagine what they look like. Here is Hammett's description of one of his characters, Joel Cairo:

> Mr. Joel Cairo was a small-boned dark man of medium height. His hair was black and smooth and very glossy. His features were Levantine. A square-cut ruby, its sides paralleled by four baguette diamonds, gleamed against the deep green of his cravat. His black coat, cut tight to narrow shoulders, flared a little over slightly plump hips. His trousers fitted his round legs more snugly than was the current fashion. The uppers of his patent-leather shoes were hidden by fawn spats. He held a black derby hat in a chamois-gloved hand and came toward Spade with short, mincing, bobbling steps. The fragrance of chypre came with him.

This description of Joel Cairo gives readers of *The Maltese Falcon* an idea of what Cairo looked like, how he was dressed and what he was like. All of the items in the description are signifiers or messages about Cairo's taste and what Hammett wants us to know about him.

A Psychoanalytic Perspective on the Mystery Story

Martin Grotjahn, a psychoanalyst, wrote a book, *Beyond Laughter: Humor and the Subconscious,* that deals not only with humor but also with other aspects of popular culture. He has a discussion of the mystery story which suggests that our interest in mysteries is much more complicated than we might imagine. As he explains (1966:153-154):

> We know that deep down in our hearts we are all murderers. We are vaguely aware of this and feel guilty; while reading a mystery story we may feel as if we did it ourselves. One part of us—the part which represents our carefully repressed hostile tendencies—identifies with the murderer while other parts of our personality identify with the detective or even with the victim who was murdered...The final victory of the moral principle over crime the punishment and atonement for crime, enjoyed vicariously and almost guilt-free, makes the reading of the mystery story a permissible enjoyment against which our conscience cannot protest.

He is arguing, in a sense, that we read mystery stories to satisfy hidden feelings about murder we all have, hidden away in the deepest recesses of our unconscious. Reading mysteries allow us to participate in the murder vicariously, and avoid feeling guilty for doing so. Mysteries are also connected, Grojahn suggests, to the interest we all had, as children, in what went on in the parental bedroom. Our fascination with mysteries is a reactivation of our interest in the primal scene and (1966:156-157):

> a reactivation of the long-repressed interest in the bloody details of life and death, intercourse, menstruation, defloration, pregnancy, birth, delivery, and all the rest of it. The secret crime is the primal scene which the child is not supposed to witness....The victim of the mystery story is usually the mother in disguise, who suffers under the cruel deeds of the tyrannical father. The criminal in our culture is usually the father.

He adds (1966:158):

> Detective-story addicts repeat the discovery of the original crime, which does not concern murder, but sex. For the rest of their life, they try to solve it.

This curiosity becomes displaced from sex to crime and the mystery story desexualizes our curiosity and channels it into a concern for justice, personified in the figure of the great detective, who can indulge in the infantile desire for uninhibited looking without any fear of reproach. Grotjahn also explains that the detective is often opposed by authorities, who represent the parents who are dumb and hinder the detective. In many detective stories, and *The Maltese Falcon* is a good example, the hero, Sam Spade, has trouble with the police who think he might be the murderer or, at the very least, know something that will help them solve the crime.

What Grotjahn writes about the mystery story can be applied to other popular culture genres which also have addictive aspects to them that help explain their popularity. We learn that what we call "taste," in this case a preference for mystery novels, or even certain kinds of mysteries, or even mysteries written by certain authors, may be connected to psychological matters and forces in the unconscious of mystery story fans of which they are unaware but which affect their behavior and taste preferences.

Chapter 15

Coda

A number of personality characteristics have been shown to be associated with creative productivity. One of these is autonomy: creative individuals tend to be independent and nonconformist in their thoughts and actions. Equally important is mastery of a particular domain—that is, a sphere of activity or knowledge that requires a high level of ability. For example, in applying their knowledge of computers to the design of the Apple II, inventors Steve Jobs and Steve Wozniak revolutionized the computer industry by appealing to individuals as well as businesses. French fashion designer Coco Chanel forever changed the way women dressed by designing simple yet stylish clothes. On the other hand, creative people may not have equally strong gifts across the spectrum of human ability. (A notable exception was Leonardo da Vinci, whose achievements in the visual arts, mechanics, and engineering disclosed the talents of a creative polymath.) Some creative people show an interest in apparent disorder, contradiction, and imbalance—perhaps because they are challenged by asymmetry and chaos. Creative individuals may also exhibit a high degree of self-assurance. Some possess an exceptionally deep, broad, and flexible awareness of themselves. Others are shown to be intellectual leaders with a great sensitivity to problems.

The unconventionality of thought that is sometimes found in creative persons may be in part a resistance to acculturation, which may be seen as demanding surrender of one's unique fundamental nature. In fact, independence is critical to the creative process, in that creative people must often be able to work alone and must also be willing to express ideas or develop products that others might perceive as radical. It should be pointed out, however, that a nonconformist lifestyle is not essential to creativity; indeed, many creative individuals lead quite ordinary lives, expressing their autonomy mainly in their unconventional ideas and work. Another trait common among creative people is that of introversion. While this does not imply a lack of social skills, it suggests that creative people tend to be reflective and inner-directed; they look to their own intuition rather than depending upon interaction with others to inform their attitudes and responses.

https://www.britannica.com/topic/creativity

Books are common objects and many people who read books or buy books (or do both) don't think much about the process of writing a book or publishing one. In this chapter, I'll say something about how I came to write a book on taste and how I wrote the book. This chapter is about the creative process.

Keeping a Journal

Like many authors, I keep a journal and in that journal, I speculate about many things, such as what subject I might want to write a book about, and I more or less carry on a conversation with myself as I write. I've been keeping a journal since 1956 and have written more than one hundred journals, and most of my books come from the thinking I did in my journal of topics that attracted me.

I have several books by Pierre Bourdieu and in one of them, he made a statement that attracted my attention. He said we have illusions that our opinions and our taste are personal when, in reality, they are socially constructed. That idea struck me as very interesting and so one day, when I was writing in a journal, I wrote, "I think I'll write a book about taste." The idea just popped into my head the way various ideas for other books have.

In that journal, I devoted many pages to brainstorming about taste and playing around with ideas about the subject. The journal page below shows my initial ideas about the structure of the book—that is, the titles of chapters, and a list of possible images to use to illustrate the book. I believe it is important to use images in books to make them more visually attractive. I am also an artist and drew most of the images used in the book, and I've also provided a few photographs when drawings wouldn't work.

I've read many comments from academics about the difficulties they face in getting their students to read textbooks, which led me to add images to make my books less threatening and to write in a reader-friendly, accessible style, to the extent possible. I also like to use many short quotations from the writers I quote so my readers will be exposed to the ideas of many great thinkers and the way they expressed themselves.

I work on three or four books at the same time, and while I am waiting to hear from an editor about a book I've written, and have a bit of free time, I start another book. Then, on page 56 of my journal, I started doing some planning about what the book would be like. I devoted the page to brainstorming about it.

Figure 15.1: Journal Chart for Taste

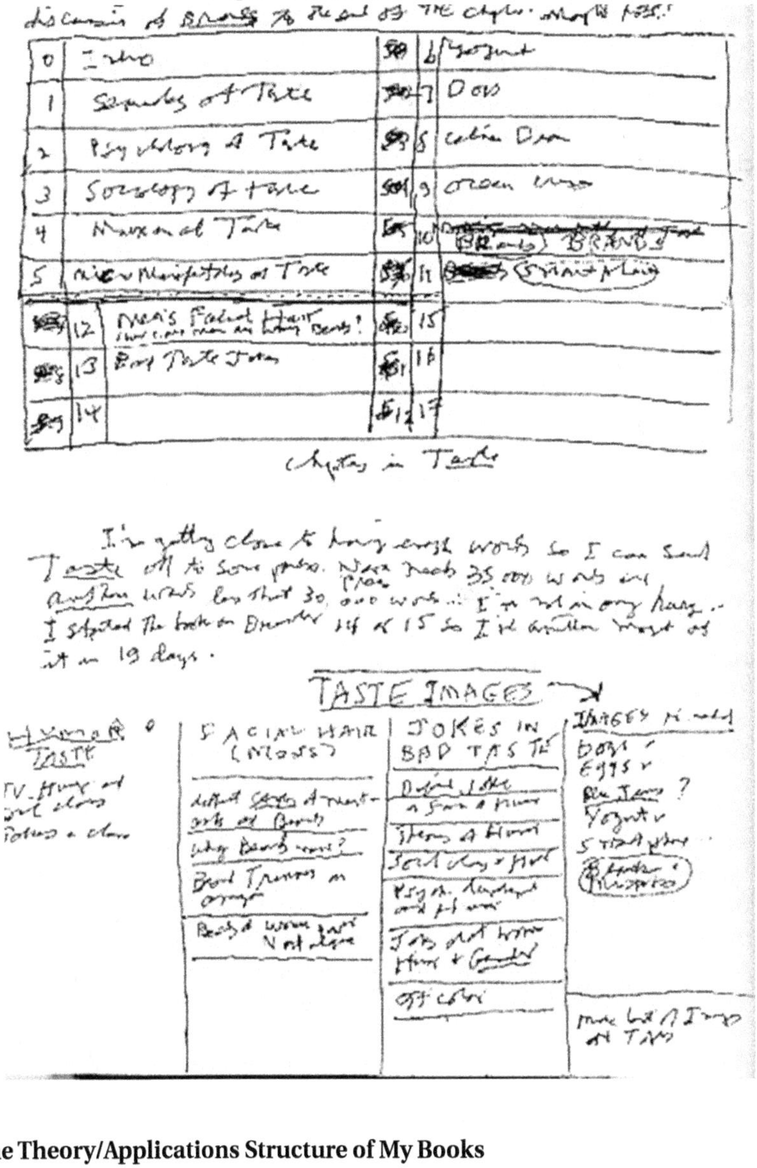

The Theory/Applications Structure of My Books

Many of my books have a similar structure. In the first part of the book, I deal with theoretical concerns and in the second part of the book, I apply the theories and concepts I've discussed to various topics. So, I did some brainstorming on the theories I would use and on the applications I might make based on the theories. I carry on this conversation with myself on quite a few pages.

Unlike some writers, who plan their books out in granular detail, when I write, my books are investigations that I make and I don't know how the book will turn out, other than in a very general way. So every book is a kind of adventure in which I move ahead one step at a time and never can be sure where I'll end up.

Figure 15.2: Brainstorming Page from Journal on Taste book

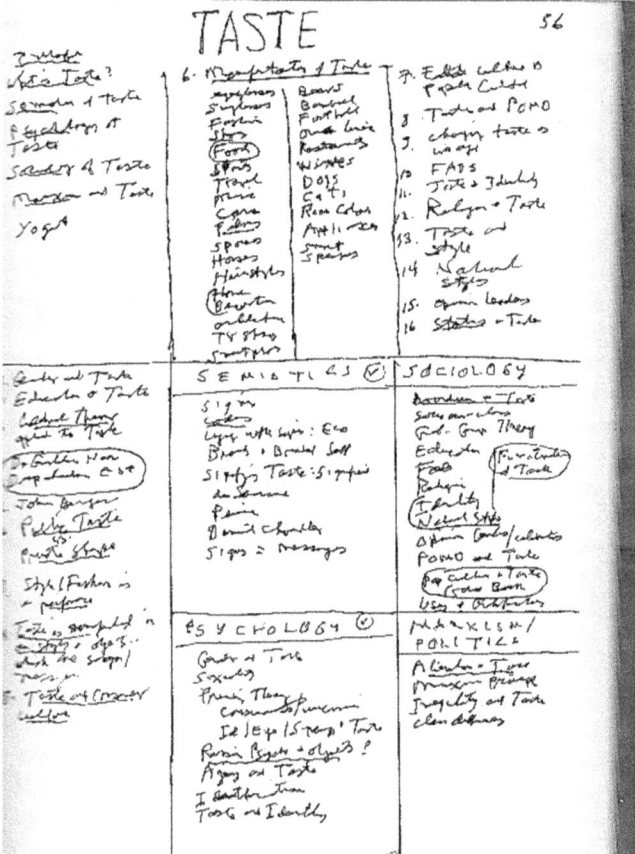

The Creative Process

As I explained earlier, when I write a book, I write notes to myself in my journal and make charts and play around with ideas. So my journals play a central role in every book I write. If you were to read one of my journals, you would find notes about each of my books and often notes about two or three books that I'm working on—off and all, at the same time.

In the material below, I deal with how I am progressing with my taste book and various topics that I hope to explore.

Figure 15.3: Journal note on Taste book

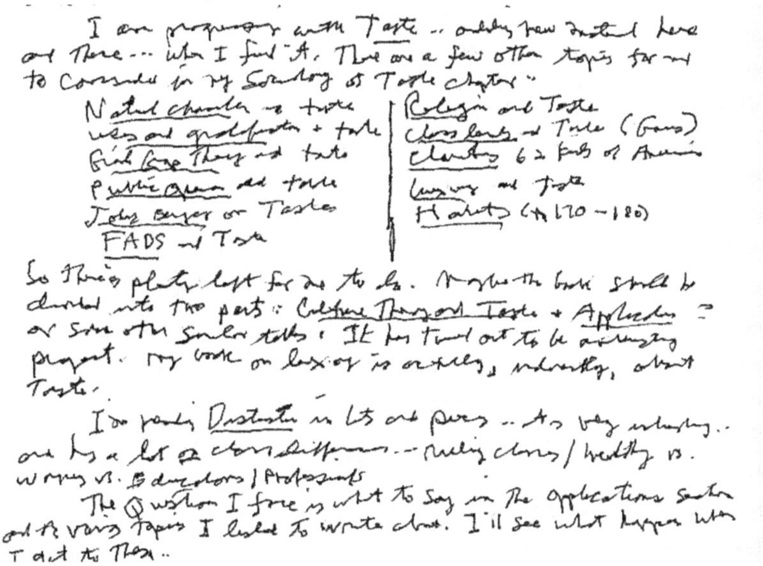

My handwriting is difficult to read, so I am rewriting part of it to show how my mind was working. In this journal note I write:

I am progressing with *Taste*...adding new material here and there...when I find it. There are a few other topics for me to consider in my sociology of taste chapter.

National Character and taste.	Religion and taste
Uses and Gratifications and taste	Class levels and taste (Gans)
Grid-Group Theory and taste	Claritas 62 kinds of Americans
Public opinion and taste	Luxury and taste
Joke analyses and taste	Habitus PM 170-180
FADS and taste	

So there is plenty left for me to do. Maybe the book should be divided into two parts: Culture Theory and Taste and Applications....

*****

Though my writing style is casual and informal, the writers and theorists whose ideas I deal with are all high-level and important thinkers. Over the years, I've made drawings of many thinkers and these drawings are found in my book on taste and in my other books, as well.

My Illustrations

I am an artist and like to illustrate my books so that they will be more visually attractive. I've had as many as sixty of my drawings, plus photos I've taken, in some books. I offer a few of my drawings below: an adolescent, a self-portrait in a crazy suit I bought while living in London and doing research on English popular culture, and a visual pun on the term "con" as in "convict."

Figure 15.4: Selected drawings by the author

Unlike many authors, I write my books before I start looking for a publisher. Many writers prepare proposals and add a chapter from a book they are planning on writing, but I don't work that way. I write the book and then start looking for a publisher. If you wait to hear from acquiring editors about book ideas you have, it can take many months. I prefer to write a book that interests me and then see what luck I have with publishers.

Thus, at any given moment, I have two or three books under review (if I'm lucky enough to find a publisher interested in a book) and that process can take months. So, while I wait to hear from publishers, I write a new book. Sometimes, of course, my manuscripts are rejected by an editor right away. At other times, the manuscript is sent off to reviewers (generally, experts on the topic of my book) whose judgment will generally determine whether the book will be published. In some cases, the reviews may be positive, but the marketing director doesn't think the book will have enough readers, so the book is rejected. So writing books is a chancy business.

Figure 15.5: One of my favorite drawings

I hope that you found *Taste* interesting and thought-provoking and that after reading this book, you will think about what taste is and how it manifests itself in your life and in society differently.

Arthur Asa Berger
Mill Valley, California

Glossary

1/6. (January 6, 2021). The date when a mob of people, apparently urged to do so by Donald Trump, invaded the Capitol, searching for people to kill, and trashed the building. This insurrection is currently being investigated by a committee in the House of Representatives, while many members of the Republican Party are redefining the event as merely a gathering of patriots and tourists, to downplay its significance.

Aberrant Decoding. The notion, elaborated by the Italian semiotician Umberto Eco, that audiences decode or interpret texts such as television commercials and print advertisements in ways that differ from the ways the creators of these texts expect them to be decoded. Aberrant decoding is the rule rather than the exception when it comes to the mass media, according to the Eco. It has been estimated that about 25 percent of advertisements and commercials are decoded aberrantly, that is, not the way the creators of the texts expected them to be decoded.

Addiction. This term, as used in the book, describes a kind of compulsive behavior people develop about their iPhones, video games they like, and digitally accessed material of all kinds.

Advertisement. The word "advert" means "to call attention to something," and thus an advertisement is, for our purposes, a kind of text—carried by electronic or print media—that attracts attention to, stimulates a desire for, and in some cases leads to the purchase of a product or service. The convention is that commercial messages in print are called advertisements and those in electronic media are called commercials.

Alienation. In Marxist theory, capitalist societies can create enormous amounts of consumer goods, but they also inevitably generate alienation and feelings of estrangement from people in themselves and others in society. Alienation is functional for those who own the means of production and distribution since alienation leads to consumer cultures—ones characterized by endless and frantic consumption, which people use as an escape from their feelings of alienation. In capitalist societies, therefore, advertising plays a central role in maintaining the status quo and distracting people from focusing their attention on the inequality in capitalist countries and engaging in revolutionary behavior.

Anomie. Durkheim used the term to describe people who don't have the norms that most people have in a given society. Anomie is different from alienation. Members of a gang may be anomic, but they don't suffer from alienation.

Apple iPhone. This phone became an international bestseller when it was introduced and remains one of the most popular and most technologically advanced smartphones.

Aristotle. He was a Greek philosopher who founded the Lyceum, the Peripatetic school of philosophy. His writings cover physics, zoology, metaphysics, logic, poetry, theatre, music, rhetoric, psychology, linguistics, economics, politics, meteorology, geology, and government.

Audience. Audiences are generally defined as collections of individuals who watch a television program, listen to a radio show, watch a film, spend time on social media or attend some kind of live artistic performance (symphony, rock band, and so on). The members of the audience may be together in one room or, in the case of television and digital media, each watches from his or her own set, tablet or phone. In technical communication terms, audiences are addressees who receive mediated texts sent by an addresser. In conversations, an audience can be one person.

Bourdieu, Pierre. He was an influential French sociologist who argued that taste is tied to our socioeconomic status or our economic and cultural capital and is shaped more by social forces than personal desires or preferences. His book, *Distinction,* is considered one of the most important books by a sociologist in recent decades. His theory of the habitus argues that the earliest experiences of children in their families play an important role in their development.

Brands. Brands create emotional ties between certain products or services and individuals who will purchase them, sometimes throughout their lives. From a semiotic perspective, brands are signs people use to display their taste or wealth and to help them fashion an identity. The fact that certain companies prominently attach their logos to what they make helps users solidify their sense of style and discrimination and their identities.

Broadway Riders. A gang of poseurs who dress like members of motorcycle gangs but do not own motorcycles.

Butler, Judith. She is a leading feminist thinker and the author of an influential book, *Gender Trouble and the Subversion of Identity.* She argues that gender is, in essence, a performance and that the bipolar opposition of male and female is no longer valid. She is a professor of rhetoric and comparative literature at the University of California at Berkeley.

Celebrity. A celebrity is someone who is well known by people for reasons that are often difficult to determine. They play a role as influencers in shaping people's consumption practices and taste preferences.

Celine Dion. She is a Canadian singer with a powerful voice who is one of the best-selling female singers of modern times. Many critics dislike her singing, arguing that her songs are overly sentimental, uncool, and liked by people with lowbrow taste. Her show in Las Vegas has been sold out for many years.

Chandler, Daniel. He is a British semiotician and author of a well-known book on semiotics, *Semiotics: The Basics.* now in its fourth edition. He has written a great deal on codes and their relation to signs in semiotic theory.

Claritas. This marketing research firm lists more than sixty kinds of Americans that advertising agencies can target as having similar tastes. It argues that "birds of a feather flock together" and members of its various categories tend to consume the same brands of products.

Class. From a linguistic standpoint, a class is any group of things that have something in common. We use the term to refer to social classes, or more literally, socioeconomic classes: groups of people who share similar status and beliefs.

Communication. We often make a distinction between communication using language, verbal communication, and communication using facial expressions, body language, and other means, or nonverbal communication. Communication involves the transfer of messages from senders to receivers.

Consumer Cultures. Consumer cultures are characterized by widespread personal consumption rather than socially conscious and useful investment in the public sphere. The focus is on private expenditure and leisure pursuits, and this leads to privatism, self-centeredness, and a reluctance to allocate resources to the public realm. Advertising is held by many critics to be a primary instrument of those who own the means of production in generating consumer lust and consumer cultures and distracting people from social and public matters. Social scientists Aaron Wildavsky and Mary Douglas suggest that there are four political cultures, which also function as consumer cultures: hierarchical or elitist, individualist, egalitarian, and fatalist. Luxury goods make up about ten percent of purchases in consumer cultures.

Culture. There are hundreds of definitions of culture. Generally speaking, from the anthropological perspective, it involves the transmission from generation to generation of specific ideas, arts, customary beliefs, ways of living, behavior patterns, institutions, and values. When applied to the arts, it generally is used to specify "elite" kinds of artworks, such as operas, poetry, classical music, novels, and "serious" art that require a certain amount of discrimination. Postmodernists do not consider "elite" culture and "popular culture" to be very different from one another.

Culture Code. A book by Clotaire Rapaille that describes consumption practices in different countries. It argues that children, up to the age of seven, become imprinted by a particular country's codes of behavior and those codes shape people's behavior for the rest of their lives. I argue in many of my writings that what we think of as a culture can be understood to be a collection of codes of behavior and thinking that people learn growing up in a culture or subculture. If you understand and can recognize people's "imprinted" codes, you can better understand their behavior.

Cultural Studies aka Cultural Criticism. The term "cultural criticism" refers to the analysis of texts and various aspects of everyday life by scholars in various disciplines who use concepts from their fields of expertise to interpret mass-mediated texts, the role of the mass media, and related concerns. The focus is on the impact of these texts and the media that carry them have on individuals, society, and culture. Cultural criticism involves the use of literary theory, media analysis, philosophical thought, communication theory, and various interpretive methodologies such as semiotics, psychoanalytic theory, Marxist theory and sociological theory.

Defense Mechanisms. According to Freudian psychoanalytic theory, Defense Mechanisms are methods used by the ego to defend itself against pressures from the id, the impulsive elements in the psyche. Some of the more common defense mechanisms are *repression* (barring unconscious instinctual wishes, memories, and so on from consciousness), *regression* (returning to earlier stages in one's development), *ambivalence* (a simultaneous feeling of love and hate for a person, thing or concept), and *rationalization* (offering excuses to justify one's actions).

Demographics. The term demographics refers to similarities found in groups of people in terms of race, religion, gender, social class, ethnicity, occupation, place of residence, age, and so on. Demographic information plays an important role in the creation of advertising and the choice of which media to use to deliver this advertising.

de Certeau, Michel. A French Jesuit priest and scholar who used psychoanalytic theory and other methodologies in his books on everyday life. He argued that people can counter with messages sent to them by elites by various subterfuges in his book, *The Practice of Everyday Life*. He also wrote *Heterologies: Discourse on the Other*, which deals with the ideas of Freud, Lacan, and Foucault.

de Saussure, Ferdinand de. He was one of the founding fathers of the science of semiotics. His book, *Course in General Linguistics*, played a major role in the development of semiotics. He called his science "semiology," which means, literally speaking, words about signs. He wrote that a sign is made up of two parts: a *signifier* (word or thing) and a *signified* (what the signifier means; that is, a concept). The relationship between a signifier and signified is arbitrary and based on convention, which means that the meanings of signs can change over time. There are, to simplify matters, two schools of semiotics: Saussure's and Peirce's.

Disfunctional (also **Dysfunctional**). In sociological thought, something is dysfunctional if it contributes to the breakdown or destabilization of the entity in which it is found. Functional theory is one of the dominant concerns of many sociologists, political scientists, and social scientists.

Douglas, Mary. She was a British social anthropologist who developed grid-group theory, which argues that the number of rules and restrictions and the strength of the boundaries of the "lifestyles" to which people belong shapes their preferences in many areas. These lifestyles are not self-conscious groups but exist in modern societies and affect people's taste, politics, and many other areas of life. In her influential article, "In Defence of Shopping," she explains: "We have to make a radical shift away from thinking about consumption as a manifestation of individual choices. Culture itself is the result of myriads of individual choices, not primarily between commodities but between kinds of relationships."

Durkheim, Emile. Durkheim was one of the most influential sociologists and is considered the father of French sociology. He is the author of a classic study of suicide, of religion, and wrote numerous other books.

Eco, Umberto. An influential Italian semiotician and novelist whose work on semiotic theory and how it can be applied to popular culture and other kinds of texts and phenomena has been very important. His extremely complex novels are popular in Europe and many other countries. His novel, *Name of the Rose* was made into a popular film.

Egalitarians. They stress that everyone is equal in terms of certain needs such as food, shelter, and access to health care. Egalitarians function as critics of the two dominant political/consumer cultures, elitist and individualist. Egalitarians are one of the four "lifestyles" discussed by social-anthropologist Mary Douglas and grid-group theorists.

Ego. In Sigmund Freud's theory of the psyche, the ego functions as the executant of the id and as a mediator between the id and the superego (conscience). The ego is involved in the perception of reality and adaptation to reality. One aspect of the ego, I suggest, is in helping the superego to restrain compulsive spending, which the id wishes to do.

Ekman, Paul. American psychologist and world-famous authority on facial expression. He argues that there are a limited number of universal facial expressions.

Enclavists. Mary Douglas' term for Egalitarians. Enclavists are one of the four lifestyles Douglas wrote about in her work on grid-group theory.

Erikson, Erik. A developmental psychoanalyst who wrote important studies of children and adolescents. He was born in Germany but practiced in America and is considered one of the most important psychologists in recent years. He argued that hat personality develops in a predetermined order through eight stages of psychosocial development, from infancy to adulthood.

Ethnomethodology. This branch of sociology deals with how social interactions shape the social order. It is interested in analyzing conversation as a key to understanding behavior. Harold Garfinkel was one of its most outstanding theorists.

False Consciousness. In Marxist thought, false consciousness refers to mistaken ideas that people have about their class, status, and economic possibilities. These ideas help maintain the status quo and are of great use to members of the ruling class, who want to avoid changes in the social and economic structure of a society. Karl Marx argued that the ideas of the ruling class are always the ruling ideas in society. Marxists would argue that the belief many Americans have that they can succeed if they have enough willpower and are "elites" because they can consume at a relatively high level, are examples of false consciousness.

Fatalists. They are at the bottom rungs of society. They have little political or consumer power and can only escape their status as a result of luck or chance, such as winning a lottery. Fatalists are one of the four "lifestyles" discussed by grid-group theorists.

Feminist Theory. Feminist theory focuses on the roles given to women and the way they are portrayed in texts of all kinds, including one of the worst offenders—advertising. Feminist critics argue that women are typically used as sexual objects and are portrayed stereotypically in advertisements and other kinds of texts, and this has negative effects on both men and women.

Jameson, Fredric. One of the most important theorists of postmodernism and the author of an influential book, *Postmodernism, or, The Cultural Logic of Late Capitalism.* Jameson argues that postmodernism is an advanced form of capitalism.

Functional. In sociological thought, the term "functional" refers to the contribution an institution makes to the maintenance of society, an institution, or entity. Something functional helps maintain the system in which it is found. Many social scientists are functionalists.

Functional Alternative. This term refers to something that takes the place of something else. For example, professional football can be seen as a functional alternative to religion. I argue in this book that a department store can be seen as a modern functional alternative to medieval cathedrals.

Gans, Herbert. An American sociologist who wrote about popular culture in America and argues that there are what he calls "taste cultures" that are appropriate for different socio-economic classes.

Gender. Gender is the sexual category of an individual and the behavioral traits that are connected to each category. Gender is now held to be "socially constructed," which means it is our societies that determine what we think about gender. The binary distinction between males and females is no longer considered valid and individuals now have a range of possibilities when defining and choosing their gender.

GOP. The GOP stands for the Grand Old Party, which is one of the ways that the Republican Party has been described. In recent years, the nature of the Republican Party has changed and the people Republicans vote into power tend to be ideological extremists. Some writers and social scientists argue that the Republican Party has become a cult whose leader is Donald Trump.

Gorer, Geoffrey. A British anthropologist who used psychoanalytic theory in his writings. He wrote about topics such as national character and the role that swaddling babies in Russia played in shaping the Russian psyche (for the people of Great Russia). He wrote books such as *The Americans, The People of Great Russia, Exploring English Character, Death, Grief, and Mourning in Contemporary Britain,* and *The Danger of Equality.*

Grid-Group Theory. This theory is based on the work of social anthropologist Mary Douglas, who argued that there are four (and only four) consumer cultures or "lifestyles" in modern societies, based on the degree to which the groups to which people belong have weak or strong boundaries and whether members of these groups have few or many rules and prescriptions to follow. The four lifestyles compete with one another and are antagonistic but also need each other.

Habitus. This concept deals with the impact of early childhood experiences on people's development. Bourdieu defines it as "a subjective but not individual system of internalized structures, schemes of perception, conception, and action common to all members of the same group or class."

Haug, Wolfgang. A German Marxist who has written extensively about consumer culture and the role of aesthetics in advertising and selling products and services to people.

Hierarchical Elitists. These people are one of the four lifestyles in Grid-Group theory and are at the top of the economic and power pyramid. They believe that hierarchy is needed for society to run smoothly, but also have a sense of obligation to those beneath them. Elitists and individualists make up the core of luxury purchasers, since they have the social and economic capital needed to buy luxury products and services.

Hypothesis. A hypothesis is essentially a guess about something. Social scientists use the term to suggest that they have ideas that may be interesting and even correct, but which they have not been able to verify. We use the term to signify that we have an interesting idea about something, but lack proof that our idea is correct.

Id. The Id in Freud's theory of the psyche (technically known as his structural hypothesis) is that element of the psyche that is the representative of a person's drives. In *New Introductory Lectures on Psychoanalysis*, Freud called it "a chaos, a cauldron of seething excitement." It also is the source of energy, but lacking direction, it needs the ego to harness it and control it. In popular thought, it is connected to impulse, lust, and "I want it all now" behavior. Many advertisements, for all kinds of products and services, appeal to Id elements in our psyches.

Ideology. A logically coherent, integrated explanation of social, economic, and political matters that helps establish the goals and direct the actions of a group or political entity. People act (and vote or don't vote) based on an ideology they hold, even though they may not have articulated it or thought about it. Some critics argue that advertising is an ideological tool that members of the ruling class use to distract people from their problems and convince them that the political order is worth supporting.

Image. Defining images is extremely difficult. In my book, *Seeing Is Believing: An Introduction to Visual Communication*, I define an image as "a collection of signs and symbols—what we find when we look at a photograph, a film still, a shot of a television screen, a print advertisement, or just about anything." The term is used for mental as well as physical representations of things. Images often have powerful emotional effects on people and are of great historical significance.

Impostor. There are two ways to understand the impostor syndrome. The first is that an impostor is someone who pretends to have an identity. Impostors are different from impersonators, who pretend to be someone in particular. The second is that impostors often feel that they are frauds and undeserving of their successes and accomplishments.

Imprints. According to the French psychoanalyst and marketing theorist Clotaire Rapaille, children in all countries are imprinted, by the age of seven, by the culture of the country in which they grow up. These imprints then shape, to a considerable degree, their thinking and behavior (and taste) when they are adults. He discusses this in his book, *Culture Codes*.

Individualists. In Grid-Group theory, individualists are members of a lifestyle that believes that the basic function of government is to prevent crime and invasion by foreign powers. They are competitive and stress the importance of individual initiative.

Intertextuality. This theory argues that texts (works of art) of all kinds are influenced to varying degrees by texts that preceded them. Sometimes, as in the case of parody, the relationship is overt, but in many cases, creators of texts are influenced by stylistic practices or thematic ones from earlier works. We can say then that intertextuality involves making allusions to, imitating, modifying, or adapting previously created texts and styles of expression. Parody is a literary style that is intertextual. Some examples of intertextuality are: Disney's *The Lion King,* which is a take on Shakespeare's *Hamlet* and J.K. Rowling's *Harry Potter* series, which makes use of T. H. White's *The Sword in the Stone*, and C. S. Lewis's *The Chronicles of Narnia*

Isolates. The term Mary Douglas uses for the lifestyle described by others as Fatalists.

Jameson, Fredric. One of the most important theorists of postmodernism and the author of an influential book, *Postmodernism, or, The Cultural Logic of Late Capitalism*. Jameson argues that postmodernism is an advanced form of capitalism.

Latent Functions. Latent functions are hidden, unrecognized, and unintended results of some activity, entity, or institution. They are contrasted by social scientists with manifest functions, which are recognized and intended. The manifest function of buying a luxury automobile may be because it is technically superior to other cars, but the latent function of buying the car is to show that one can afford it and to gain status.

Lifestyle. Literally style of life, lifestyle refers to the way people live, to the decisions they make about how to decorate their homes (and where the homes are located), the cars they drive, the clothes they wear, the foods they eat, the restaurants they visit, and where they go for vacations. Lifestyles tend to be coherent or logically connected, and they play an important part in market research because lifestyles tend to shape consumption patterns in individuals. Social anthropologist Mary Douglas, in an article on shopping, uses the term to describe the four kinds of consumers found in contemporary societies: elitist, individualist, egalitarian, and fatalist. She argues that people's lifestyles play an important role in determining their preferences in many areas of life in consumption cultures.

LGBTQIA+. The letters stand for Lesbian, Gay, Bisexual, Transgender, Queer/ Questioning, Intersexual, Asexual/Aromantic, and other identities in Queerness— all of which are possibilities in non-binary gender identities that people can assume.

Lyotard, Jean-François. Lyotard was a French critic and writer whose book, *The Postmodern Condition,* is an important primer for anyone interested in postmodernism.

Manifest Functions. The manifest functions of an activity, entity, or institution are those that are obvious and intended. Manifest functions contrast with latent functions, which are hidden and unintended. The manifest function of advertising is to sell products and services; the latent function is to sell the political order. See also Latent Functions.

Mass Communication. This term refers to the transfer of messages, information, and texts from a sender to receivers, in many cases a large number of people, a mass audience. This transfer is done through the technologies of the mass media—newspapers, magazines, television programs, films, records, computers, the Internet, and CD-ROMs. A sender is often a person in a large media organization, the messages are public, and the audience tends to be large and varied. With the development of social media such as Facebook and Instagram, now many people can communicate with large numbers of others.

Medium (plural: Media). A medium is a means of delivering messages, information, or texts to audiences. There are different ways of classifying the media. One of the most common is as follows: print (newspapers, magazines, books, billboards), electronic (radio, television, computers, CD-ROMs, the Internet), and photographic (photographs, films, videos). Various critics have suggested that the main function of commercial media is to deliver audiences to advertisers and that everything else the media does is of secondary importance.

Metaphor. A metaphor is a figure of speech that conveys meaning by analogy. For example, "My love is a rose." It is important to realize that metaphors are not confined to poetry and literary works but, according to some linguists, are the fundamental way in which we make sense of things and find meaning in the world. A simile is a weaker form of metaphor that uses either "like" or "as" in making an analogy. Metaphors are an important element in advertising. For example, Fidji perfume had a campaign that was explicitly metaphorical: "Woman is an island." If the advertisement had said "Woman is like an island," that would have been a simile.

Metonymy. According to linguists, metonymy is a figure of speech that conveys information by association and is, along with metaphor, one of the most important ways people convey information to one another. We tend not to be aware of our use of metonymy, but whenever we use association to get an idea about something (Rolls-Royce signifies wealth) we are thinking metonymically. A form of metonymy that involves seeing a whole in terms of a part or vice versa is called synecdoche. Using the Pentagon to stand for the American military is an example of synecdoche.

Modernism. The period before postmodernism, from roughly 1900 to 1960, when postmodernism became culturally dominant. Modernism's esthetics and values, its belief in master narratives (like its belief in progress), and grand theories were rejected by postmodernist thinkers and people affected by postmodernist thought.

Myth. Myths are conventionally understood to be sacred stories about gods and cultural heroes (and in more recent years, mass-mediated heroes and heroines) that are used to transmit a culture's basic belief system to younger generations and to explain natural and supernatural phenomena. This book argues that myths play an important role in shaping our behavior in many areas of life, which I describe in what I call the "myth model." This model argues that myths inform many aspects of our lives, though we may not recognize this is the case. It shows how myths can be found in psychoanalytic theory, historical experience, elite culture, popular culture, and everyday life.

National character. This theory argues that people who grow up in a country can be characterized by sharing certain values, beliefs, and distinctive behaviors. Thus, there is a big difference between people in different countries—a topic explored by Clotaire Rapaille in his book, *The Culture Code*, and the work of the anthropologist Geoffrey Gorer and countless other social scientists and writers.

Nonfunctional. In sociological thought, something is nonfunctional if it is neither functional nor dysfunctional and plays no role in the entity in which it is found.

Nonverbal Communication. Our body language, facial expressions, styles of dress, and hairstyles are examples of our communicating feelings and attitudes (and a sense of who we are) without words. In our everyday lives, a great deal of our communication is done nonverbally. It is estimated that between sixty percent to ninety percent of the messages we send to others are nonverbal in nature.

Ocean Cruising. It is an increasingly important form of tourism with lines that appeal to people of different incomes and tastes. Cruises can cost as little as $50 a day per person to $1000 a day or more per person on some luxury cruise lines and specialty excursion ships.

Pappenheim, Fritz. A German Marxist who wrote about the importance of alienation in Marxist theory and the impact of alienation on life in capitalist countries.

Peirce, Charles Sanders. One of the founding fathers of the study of signs, who gave the science its name, semiotics, a term based on the Greek word for sign, sēmeîon. He was a professor at Harvard and produced many seminal works on semiotic theory.

Phallic Symbol. In Freudian theory, an object that resembles the penis either by shape or function is described as a phallic symbol. Symbolism is a defense mechanism of the ego that permits hidden or repressed sexual or aggressive thoughts to be expressed in a disguised form. For a discussion of this topic, see Freud's book, *An Interpretation of Dreams.* I offer the example of the Washington Monument as a gigantic phallic symbol, named after the father of our country. The term, "phallocentric" is used to suggest societies that are dominated by males, and the ultimate source of this domination, which shapes our institutions and cultures, is the male phallus. In this theory, a link is made between the male sexual organ and male power.

Pines, Maya. American journalist and author of an article on semiotics discussed in this book. She explained that what semioticians call signs should be seen as messages conveying meaning.

Popular. Popular is one of the most difficult terms used in discourse about the arts and the media. The term means, "appealing to a large number of people." It comes from the Latin *popularis,* which means "of the people." Separating the popular and elite arts has become increasingly problematic in recent years and the idea that they are radically different has been rejected by postmodern theorists. For example, is an opera shown on television an example of elite or popular culture?

Popular Culture. Popular culture is a term that identifies certain kinds of texts, generally mass-mediated, that appeal to large numbers of people. But mass communication theorists often identify "popular" with "mass" and suggest that if something is popular, it must be of poor quality, appealing to the mythical "lowest common denominator." Popular culture is generally held to be the opposite of elite culture—arts that require certain levels of sophistication and refinement to be appreciated, such as ballet, opera, poetry, and classical music. Many critics now question this popular culture/elite culture polarity.

Postmodernism. This theory states that a new kind of culture has developed in the United States and elsewhere, since approximately 1960, which rejected the values and beliefs of the modernist society that had been dominant until that time. One theorist of postmodernism, Lyotard, argued that it involves "incredulity toward metanarratives," by which he means the rejection of the overarching religious, social, political, aesthetic, and moral theories of the modernist period that had shaped people's thinking and their lives. Postmodernism is associated with stylistic eclecticism and a rejection of the split between elite and popular culture. The theory is very controversial and important facets of it are explored in my books, *Postmortem for a Postmodernist* (a postmodern mystery) and *The Portable Postmodernist.*

Psychoanalytic Theory. Sigmund Freud can be said to be the founding father of psychoanalytic theory. He argued that the human psyche had three levels: consciousness, preconsciousness, and the unconscious, which is the largest area of the psyche and an area not able to be accessed by individuals. What is important, psychoanalytic theorists argue, is that the unconscious shapes and affects our mental functioning and our behavior. Another of his theories posited three forces in the psyche: the id (desire), the ego (reason), and the superego (guilt), which are continually battling with one another for domination. Freud believed that sexuality and what he called "the Oedipus Complex" play a dominant role in human behavior, even if their presence is not recognized.

Psychographics. In marketing, the term "psychographics" is used to deal with groups of people who have similar psychological characteristics or profiles. It differs from demographics, which marketers use to focus on social and economic characteristics that people have in common.

Qanon. It is a cult that believes a cabal of Satan-worshipping cannibalistic pedophiles in the Democratic party run a global child sex-trafficking ring and plots against Donald Trump, who leads the fight against the cabal.

Rapaille, Clotaire. French psychoanalyst and marketer who wrote *The Culture Code* and *The Global Code,* books that deal with how different nationalities and how new global elites shape purchasing decisions. He argued that children up to the age of seven are imprinted with the meaning of things most central to our lives and that different countries imprint different codes upon children.

Rationalization. In Freudian thought, a rationalization is a defense mechanism of the ego that creates an excuse to justify an action (or inaction when an action is expected). Ernest Jones, who introduced the term, used it to describe logical and rational reasons that people give to justify behavior that is really caused by unconscious and irrational determinants. We often use rationalizations to justify purchases that are unwise and unnecessary.

Regent Seven Seas. An ultra-luxury cruise line whose brochure's use of superlatives was discussed in this book.

Riviera, Joan. A British psychoanalyst and a founding member of the British Psychoanalytical Society, and editor of *the International Journal of Psycho-Analysis* from 1920 until 1937. She translated Freud's work into English. Riviere co-authored a book with another British psychoanalyst, Melanie Klein, *Love, Hate and Reparation.* Her contribution to the book was titled, "Hate, Greed and Aggression." The book is based on public lectures given in March 1936 about "The Emotional Life of Civilized Men and Women."

Role. Sociologists describe a role as a way of behavior that is appropriate to a particular situation. A person generally plays many roles with different people during the hours of a day, such as parent (family), worker (job), and spouse (marriage). We also use the term to describe the parts actors have in plays, films, and mass-mediated narratives, including commercials.

Rubinstein, Ruth P. American sociologist of fashion and clothing and author of *Dress Codes: Meaning and Messages in American Culture.*

Sapirstein, Milton. An American psychiatrist who has written about the psychological significance of different aspects of everyday life such as decorating a home or relying on marriage manuals.

Self. This term is very difficult to define and because of that, there are countless definitions of the concept. Generally, a self is held to refer to a coherent sense of identity and a recognition of the ways that although we are in many respects like others, we also are all different from everyone else.

Semiotics. Literally, the term "semiotics" means "the science of signs." Sēmeîon is the Greek term for sign. A sign is anything that can be used to stand for anything else. According to C. S. Peirce, one of the founders of the science, a sign "is something which stands to somebody for something in some respect or capacity." Semiotics is one of the core disciplines used by cultural studies scholars.

Sign. The basic concept in semiotics, the science of signs (from the Greek word sēmeîon, sign) that deals with how we find meaning in images and other kinds of communication. Ferdinand de Saussure, one of the founding fathers of semiotics, argued that a sign is made up of a *signifier* (a sound or object) and a *signified* (a concept). The relation between the signifier and the signified is arbitrary and not natural. C. S. Peirce, another founding father of semiotics, had a different notion. He said a sign is "something which stands to somebody for something in some respect or capacity." His theory of signs is dealt with in the discussion of symbols.

Simmel, Georg. A German sociologist and philosopher who wrote on culture and society and whose ideas led to the development of urban sociology. Because he was Jewish, he never obtained a chair in an important German university, but his writings have been very influential, especially for non-positivist sociologists.

Social Control. Social controls are ideas, beliefs, values, and more people get from their societies that shape their beliefs and behavior. People are both individuals with certain distinctive physical and emotional characteristics and desires, and, at the same time, members of societies. People's beliefs, values, and tastes are shaped by the institutions found in these societies.

Socialization. Socialization refers to the processes by which societies teach individuals how to behave: what rules to obey, roles to assume, and values to hold. Socialization was traditionally done by the family, educators, religious figures, and peers. The mass media in general and advertising, in particular, seem to have usurped this function to a considerable degree nowadays, with consequences that are not always positive.

Socioeconomic Class. A socioeconomic class is a categorization of people according to their incomes and related social status and lifestyles. In Marxist thought, there are ruling classes that shape the consciousness of the working classes (the proletariat), and history is, in essence, a record of class conflict.

Spectacle. The focus on spectacle is found in the book, *The Society of the Spectacle*, by Guy Debord. He argues that capitalist societies are shaped by spectacles and the triumph of images and illusion over reality.

Stereotypes. Stereotypes are commonly held, simplistic, and inaccurate group portraits of categories of people. Stereotypes can be positive, negative, or mixed, but generally, they are negative. Stereotyping involves making gross overgeneralizations. (All Mexicans, Chinese, Jews, African-Americans, WASPS, Americans, lawyers, doctors, professors, and so on, are held to have certain characteristics, usually negative.)

Subculture. Any complex society is made up of numerous subcultures that differ from the dominant culture in terms of such matters as ethnicity, race, religion, sexual orientation, beliefs, values, and tastes. Often members of subcultures are marginalized and victimized by members of the dominant culture.

Superego. In Freud's structural hypothesis, the superego is the agency in our psyches related to conscience and morality. The superego is involved with processes such as approval and disapproval of wishes based on their morality, critical self-observation, and a sense of guilt over wrongdoing. The functions of the superego are largely unconscious and are opposed to id elements in our psyches. Mediating between the two and trying to balance them are our egos.

Swift, Jonathan. British satirist and author of *Gulliver's Travels*. One of the most important writers of his era, he is remembered for works such as *A Tale of a Tub* (1704), *An Argument Against Abolishing Christianity* (1712), *Gulliver's Travels* (1726), and *A Modest Proposal* (1729). The *Britannica* describes Swift as the foremost prose satirist in the English language.

Symbol. Literally speaking, a symbol is something that stands for something else. The term comes from the Greek word *symballein,* which means "to put together." Advertisers use symbols because they have powerful emotional effects on people. Think, for example, of all that is found in three symbols: the cross, the Star of David, and the crescent. In C.S. Peirce's theory of semiotics, there are three kinds of signs: icons, which communicate by resemblance; indexes, which communicate by cause and effect; and symbols, whose meaning must be learned.

Taste. This term, the core subject of this book, generally is understood to involve people's liking of things, the sense people have that some article of clothing looks good, some kind of food tastes delicious and other areas where choice is a factor and one's choice demonstrates one's attitudes and feelings about something. As Pierre Bourdieu explains in his book, *Distinction* (1984:1) "Whereas the ideology of charisma regards taste in legitimate culture as a gift of nature, scientific observation shows that cultural needs are the product of upbringing and education...and preferences in literature, painting, or music, are closely linked to educational level (measured by qualifications or length of schooling) and secondarily to social origin."

Text. For our purposes, a text is, broadly speaking, any work of art in any medium. Critics use the term "text" as a convenience—so they don't have to name a given work all the time or use various synonyms. There are problems involved in deciding what the text is when we deal with serial texts, such as soap operas or comics. This book uses the term to stand for literary works, popular culture works, and any other kind of advertising or commercial messages carried by any medium.

Theory. I make a distinction between theories and concepts. Theories, as I use the term, are expressed in language and systematically and logically attempt to explain and predict phenomena being studied. They differ from concepts, which define phenomena that are being studied, and from models, which are abstract, usually graphic, and explicit about what is being studied. For example, Freud developed psychoanalytic theory and one of the concepts in this theory is what he called the unconscious.

Typology. We will understand a typology to be a system of classification that is done to clarify matters. Typologies are important because they allow us to organize ideas and concepts and we can use them to see relationships of interest.

Uses and Gratifications. This sociological theory argues that researchers should pay attention to the way audiences use the media (or certain texts or genres of texts, such as soap operas, romance novels, print advertisements, mysteries, and other similar texts) and the gratifications they get from their use of these texts and the media. Uses and gratifications researchers focus on how audiences use the media and not on how the media affects audiences.

Values. Values are abstract and general beliefs or judgments about what is right and wrong, and what is good and bad, that have implications for individual behavior and social, cultural, and political entities. There are some problems with values from a philosophical point of view. First, how does one determine which values are correct and good and which aren't? That is, how do we justify values? Are values objective or subjective? Second, what happens when there is a conflict between groups, each of which holds a central value that conflicts with that of another group?

Warren, W. Lloyd. An anthropologist and sociologist whose work on social class in the United States was of major importance. He elaborated a famous typology which argued that there are six classes in America: upper-upper, lower upper, upper-middle, lower-middle, upper lower and lower-lower, with lower-middle and upper-lower forming the "common man" (and now common woman) level.

Weber, Max. One of the most influential sociologists and thinkers in recent years and regarded as one of the fathers of sociology along with Auguste Comte, Karl Marx, and Émile Durkheim, Weber saw himself not as a sociologist but as a historian. Unlike Émile Durkheim, Weber did not believe in mono-causal explanations, proposing instead that for any outcome, there can be multiple causes. Weber's main intellectual concern was in understanding the processes of rationalization and secularization. He argued that these processes result from a new way of thinking about the world and are associated with the rise of capitalism and modernity.

Youth Culture Youth cultures are subcultures formed by young people around some area of interest, usually connected with leisure and entertainment, such as rock music, computer games, hacking, and so on. Typically, youth cultures adopt distinctive ways of dressing and develop institutions that cater to their needs.

About the Author

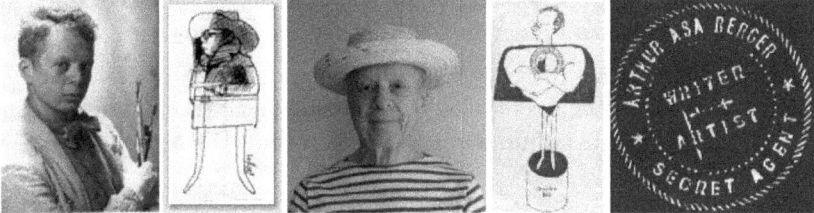

Arthur Asa Berger is Professor Emeritus of Broadcast and Electronic Communication Arts at San Francisco State University, where he taught between 1965 and 2003. He graduated in 1954 from the University of Massachusetts, where he majored in literature and philosophy. He received an MA degree in journalism and creative writing from the University of Iowa in 1956. He was drafted shortly after graduating from Iowa and served in the US Army in the Military District of Washington in Washington DC, where he was a feature writer and speechwriter in the District's Public Information Office. He also wrote about high school sports for *The Washington Post* on weekend evenings while in the army.

Berger spent a year touring Europe after he was released from the Army and then went to the University of Minnesota, where he received a Ph.D. in American Studies in 1965. He wrote his dissertation on the comic strip, *Li'l Abner.* In 1963-64, he had a Fulbright to Italy and taught at the University of Milan. He spent a year as a visiting professor at the Annenberg School for Communication at The University of Southern California in Los Angeles in 1984 and two months in the fall of 2007 as a visiting professor at the School of Hotel and Tourism at the Hong Kong Polytechnic University. He spent a month lecturing at Jinan University in Guangzhou and two weeks lecturing at Tsinghua University in Beijing in Spring, 2009. He has lectured are many universities all over the world.

He is the author of more than one hundred articles published in the United States and abroad, numerous book reviews, and more than 90 books on the mass media, popular culture, humor, tourism, and everyday life. Among his books are *Bloom's Morning; The Academic Writer's Toolkit: A User's Manual; Media Analysis Technique; Seeing is Believing: An Introduction to Visual Communication; Ads, Fads And Consumer Culture; The Art of Comedy Writing;* and *Shop 'Til You Drop: Consumer Behavior and American Culture.* Berger is also an artist and has illustrated many of his books.

He has also written many comic academic mysteries such as *Postmortem for a Postmodernist, Mistake in Identity, The Mass Comm Murders: Five Media Theorists Self-Destruct,* and *Durkheim is Dead: Sherlock Holmes is Introduced to Sociological Theory.* His books have been translated into German, Italian, Russian, Arabic, Swedish, Korean, Turkish and Chinese, and he has lectured in more than a dozen countries in the course of his career.

Berger is married, has two children and four grandchildren, and lives in Mill Valley, California. He enjoys traveling and listening to classical music. He can be reached by e-mail at arthurasaberger@gmail.com.

Index of Names

A

Aristotle, 111
Arsel, Zeynep, 44
Auden, W.H., 25-26, xviii

B

Bakhtin, Mikhail, xxii
Barthelme, Donald, 53
Barthelme, Frederic, 54
Barthes, Roland, 8
Bean, Jonathan, 44
Bell, Matthew, 78
Best, Steven, 3
Blumler, A.G., 40
Bourdieu, Pierre, 2, 3, 31-32, 76-77, 126, xvii
Brenner, Charles, 20, 23
Brooks, David, 98
Burroughs, William, 53
Butler, Judith, 30, xix

C

Campbell, C., 39
Calvino, Italo, 54
Cawelti, John, 118
Chandler, Daniel, 10, xxii
Chauvin, Derek, 100
Cho, Hyun, 99

D

Dion, Celine, 73-76, 79
Douglas, Mary, 38-40, xxi
Durkheim, Emile, 35

E

Eco, Umberto, 14, xxi
Ekman, Paul, 15-16
Eliade, Mircea, 28
Ellis, Richard, 38
Emerson, Jim, 74
Erikson, Erik, 24-25, xvii-xviii

F

Falk, Pasi, 39
Featherstone, Mike, 104
Foster, David, 74
Foucault, Michel, 106, xvii
Freud, Sigmund, 20, 22, 111, xviii
Frisby, David, 104
Fromm, Erich, 49, xix

G

Gans, Herbert, 42-44, xx
Gini, Al, 115
Gitlin, Todd, 53-54
Glass, Philip, 53
Goldncr, Charles R, 80
Gorer, Geoffrey, 26-27, 37-38, xviii
Gottdiener, Mark, 10
Graves, Michael, 53
Greenberg, David, 32-33
Grotjahn, Martin, 122-123
Gurevich, M., 40

H

Hammett, Dashiell, 121
Hargrave, Sean, 88

V

W

Z

Index of Topics

www.ingramcontent.com/pod-product-compliance
Lightning Source LLC
Chambersburg PA
CBHW062031270326
41929CB00014B/2401